MASTERING
GENEALOGICAL PROOF

NATIONAL GENEALOGICAL SOCIETY
SPECIAL TOPICS SERIES

MASTERING GENEALOGICAL PROOF

By **Thomas W. Jones**

NATIONAL GENEALOGICAL SOCIETY SPECIAL TOPICS SERIES
MASTERING GENEALOGICAL PROOF

NGS Special Publication No. 107
ISBN No. 978-1-935815-07-5

Printed in the United States on chlorine-free, acid-free, 30 percent post-consumer recycled paper.

Cover photos contributed by B. Darrell Jackson and Thomas W. Jones. Author's photo courtesy of Marilyn Markham.

PUBLISHED BY
  National Genealogical Society
  3108 Columbia Pike, Suite 300
  Arlington, VA 22204-4304

In loving memory of Julie Kay Jones and to our beloved son, Tommy

Contents

List of Tables

List of Figures

Preface

All of us tracing a family's history face a paradox. We strive to reconstruct relationships and lives of people we cannot see, but if we cannot see them, how do we know we have portrayed them accurately? Is determining ancestry that predates living people's memory just guesswork? Or do we blindly trust every source we examine and ignore inconsistencies? Should we perhaps do the opposite—mistrust sources to the point that our conclusions are mostly tentative? Can we not determine reliably which genealogical findings reflect the past? If we can make that determination, how can we demonstrate its credibility to family members and other researchers?

Family historians in the twentieth century adapted concepts from the field of law to address these questions and to assess genealogical research outcomes. Recognizing the shortcomings of applying one discipline's standards to another, the Board for Certification of Genealogists distilled the field's best practices for determining accuracy into an overarching standard and labeled it "Genealogical Proof Standard," often called "the GPS." In 2000 the board published the standard in its *Genealogical Standards Manual* and delineated fifty-six research standards supporting it.

With the *Standards Manual* in print, the genealogy field took a great step forward, but family historians wanted more. Since the *Manual*'s publication practitioners have sought more guidance in implementing the GPS's five elements, including its "reasonably exhaustive search" and "soundly reasoned, coherently written conclusion." Similarly, increasing numbers of intermediate and advanced genealogy students have wanted more information about the GPS. Its use also would enhance the work of the burgeoning legions of new family historians beginning to learn about genealogical methods and standards. Every family historian—and the field as a whole—benefits when genealogical findings meet standards of accuracy.

This book is written to help researchers, students, and new family historians understand and use the GPS. It is a textbook on genealogical methodology and reasoning. Unlike many texts, however, it is written in the first person: *We* and *our* refer collectively to you, the reader, and to me, the author.

The book's arrangement resembles that of a mathematics textbook. Content is broken into digestible chunks, and the chapters use many examples to explain sets of related concepts. Each chapter concludes with a group of exercises—questions and problems that provide practice essential to mastering the chapter's content. Answers are at the back of the book.

All the exercises and nearly all the examples use real records, real research, and real issues. To the extent possible in a textbook format, examples and exercises appear in contexts showing readers the relationships among research activities, finished research products, and concepts of evidence and proof. The book concludes with a sixty-seven-item glossary of the book's technical terms, an extensive annotated bibliography and reading list, and appendixes containing two complete articles to be used for many of the book's sixty-two exercises.

Nearly all this book's examples and exercises come from research on my son's ancestry—American with British, Germanic, and Irish roots. The principles, however, are universal. Researchers use the GPS to determine identities and relationships beyond the United States and Western Europe. For examples, see many issues of the *National Genealogical Society Quarterly*, which—like other publications—has published outstanding examples of research applying the GPS to families with diverse ethnicities and geographic origins.[1]

When I began tracing my family's history, almost a half-century ago, I gave no thought to accuracy. Trusting what I read and what people sent or told me, I naively shared false information with relatives and other researchers. A few years later my research nearly ended because I mistakenly believed that my many genealogical brick walls were permanent barriers. Decades of inefficient self-educating and eventually studying articles in the *National Genealogical Society Quarterly*, attending national genealogy conferences, and having my research critiqued by others finally taught me otherwise. I began to understand genealogical evidence and proof and to use that

---

1. For an African American example, see Curtis G. Brasfield, "Tracing Slave Ancestors: Batchelor, Bradley, Branch, and Wright of Desha County, Arkansas," *NGS Quarterly* 92 (March 2004): 6–30. For a Canadian example, see Alison Hare, "Searching for Greens at the Time of Peter Robinson," *NGS Quarterly* 95 (March 2007): 17–26. For a French Canadian example, see George Findlen, "Using French-Canadian Catholic Parish Records to Establish a Missing Kinship Relationship," *NGS Quarterly* 96 (March 2008): 39–46. For a Jewish example, see Teri Tillman, "Using Indirect Evidence and Linguistic Analysis to Trace Polin Ries of New Orleans," *NGS Quarterly* 99 (December 2011): 245–74. For a Spanish example, see Peggy Ryskamp, "Tracing the Llavina Costa Family of Catalonia, Spain: Unexpected Findings in an Unexpected Source," *NGS Quarterly* 96 (June 2008): 121–28. Other authors have provided similarly competent examples of using the GPS to study families of diverse ethnicities and geopolitical areas.

knowledge to reconstruct long-forgotten lineages and biographies as accurately as I could.

I wrote this book to help other genealogists understand in a reasonable time frame what decades of trial-and-error experiences have taught me. I hope the text and exercises will save them from the embarrassing blunders and misconceptions I have experienced. I hope it will enable many more family historians to advance their genealogical research goals efficiently and accurately. All of us should be able to reconstruct confidently, and portray accurately, the lives and relationships of people we cannot see.

I thank Kay Haviland Freilich, CG, CGL; Karen Mauer Green, CG; Alison Hare, CG; Elizabeth Shown Mills, CG, CGL, FASG, FNGS; and Patricia Walls Stamm, CG, CGL.[2] They each reviewed the entire manuscript and provided valuable corrections and suggestions. I also thank the many anonymous reviewers who critiqued all or parts of it. All their comments were helpful, although any errors that remain are my own. I am most grateful to Elizabeth Mills, who over the past three decades has directly and by example taught me most of the principles this book articulates, and from whom I continue to learn. I also thank the genealogy students at Boston University and the Salt Lake Institute of Genealogy, who helped me understand how to teach the concepts this book covers.

---

2. The initials CG and CGL and the credentials they represent, Certified Genealogist and Certified Genealogical Lecturer, are service marks of the Board for Certification of Genealogists® used under license by certificants who meet genealogical competency standards prescribed for the board's programs. The postnominal FASG designates fellows of the American Society of Genealogists, who are elected on the basis of their published genealogical scholarship. The initials FNGS identify genealogists who have been named fellows of the National Genealogical Society for their service to the society or the field.

Chapter 1

Genealogy's Standard of Proof

Genealogists call acceptable conclusions "proved." Other disciplines use different terms to describe acceptability, but genealogy's standards for proof resemble those of other disciplines.

What is genealogy?

Genealogy is a research field concerned primarily with accurately reconstructing forgotten or unknown identities and relationships. Many of these identities and relationships existed in the past, but genealogical research also includes living people. Genealogy emphasizes biological and marital kinships, but it also addresses adoptive, extramarital, and other kinds of relationships within and across generations.

Genealogy is a multidisciplinary endeavor. Its knowledge base borrows from fields like anthropology, economics, genetics, history, law, mathematics, and sociology. Genealogists use sources created for business, demographic, governmental, journalistic, legal, medical, religious, social, and other purposes. As a research discipline, genealogy has its own skill set and standards. Like mathematics—a technical field supporting economics, engineering, and physics—genealogy is a problem-solving discipline in its own right and one that supports other fields, including history, law, and medicine.

Many people pursue family for pleasure and to learn more about their family's background. Enjoyment, of course, does not require accuracy. Most family historians, however, consider accurate results important. They desire a way to differentiate correct from incorrect information, to determine unspecified relationships, and to demonstrate that their research results are credible. The Genealogical Proof Standard (GPS) meets this need. It also reflects this discipline's skill set. Applicable to family history research across geopolitical boundaries, societies, languages, and time, the GPS helps us produce trustworthy family histories, enabling future generations to build upon our work. It also gives genealogists and consumers of genealogical research a framework for assessing research results.

Why a genealogical proof standard?

Research establishes conclusions that advance knowledge. In this regard genealogy is no different from other disciplines. We focus on forgotten or hidden identities, relationships, and activities of families and individuals.

Every research field has standards differentiating acceptable from unacceptable conclusions. Accommodating the possibility that an acceptable conclusion may later be overturned, each discipline's standards stop short of absolute certainty.

Genealogy has a long history of using single sources as "proofs" of names, dates, places, relationships, and other bits of genealogical data, but the practice is risky. All kinds of genealogical sources contain misinformation. The errors may be accidents of hearing, interpreting, memory, reading, or writing. They also can be intentional. Factors like carelessness, economic gain, social standing, and desires to bury unsavory information, to tell an interesting story, or simply to hide ignorance cause people reporting information to omit, distort, and invent. Avowals of truth and certifications of accuracy do not mean the information is correct. No source is trustworthy in and of itself. Like all researchers, genealogists require a multi-faceted standard to separate acceptable information items and conclusions from those that are unacceptable.

Genealogists call acceptable conclusions "proved." Other disciplines use different terms to describe acceptability, but genealogy's standards for proof resemble those of other disciplines. All research disciplines, including genealogy, encourage practitioners to revisit their own and other researchers' conclusions, especially when new findings arise. These reassessments sometimes result in rejecting and replacing previously accepted conclusions.

Proof may be more important to genealogists than other researchers because genealogical conclusions may be more vulnerable to error:

- Genealogists are not empirical scientists, who gather data by observing phenomena as they occur. Instead, we interpret evidence items from the past that have survived to the present. This evidence, much of it fragmentary and some of it erroneous, comes from sources that were imperfect the day they were created.

- Genealogy's knowledge base and skill set are comparable to those of disciplines with graduate-level curricula at reputable colleges and universities. Although genealogy is beginning to acquire academic recognition, few institutions of higher education offer it as an accredited field of study.

- Several kinds of organizations offer genealogical education, but their offerings often are targeted to beginners or offer fragmentary coverage of genealogical sources and methods. Family historians find less-basic courses difficult to locate or access.

- Many genealogical research results in print and online seem untrustworthy. Most may be correct, but their accuracy is invisible. When genealogical compilations offer little or no documentation, biography, or explanation, users cannot assess their accuracy or detect their errors.

- Researchers in many nongenealogical fields use large data sets. Random errors in such data tend to negate each other, and an error in one observation will not affect the overall pattern or trend under study. Genealogists, however, focus on one person and relationship at a time, often with limited data. One error can alter a research outcome.

A rigorous proof standard helps genealogists avoid error. Adhering to the GPS gives us results that are as reliable as possible. When we apply a proof standard to others' findings we minimize the risk of polluting our sound research with their dubious conclusions. When we explain our reasoning and show our documentation, others can see that our conclusions are reliable. A universal standard also gives us a shared framework for understanding genealogical methods and reasoning.

The Genealogical Proof Standard

Genealogy's standards for proof evolved throughout the twentieth century.[1] In 1997–2000 the Board for Certification of Genealogists codified them into the Genealogical Proof Standard (GPS).[2] The standard has five components:

1. Thorough ("reasonably exhaustive") searches in sources that might help answer a research question

2. Informative ("complete, accurate") citations to the sources of every information item contributing to the research question's answer

3. Analysis and comparison ("correlation") of the relevant sources and information to assess their usefulness as evidence of the research question's answer

4. Resolution of any conflicts between evidence and the proposed answer to a research question

5. A written statement, list, or narrative supporting the answer[3]

The standard's five parts are interdependent. For example, source citations (element 2) reflect research scope (element 1) and analysis (element 3).

---

1. For the evolution of genealogical standards of accuracy, see David L. Greene, "Donald Lines Jacobus, Scholarly Genealogy, and *The American Genealogist*," in *The American Genealogist* 72 (July/October 1997): 159–80. Also, Harry Macy Jr., "Recognizing Scholarly Genealogy and Its Importance to Genealogists and Historians," *New England Historical and Genealogical Register* 150 (January 1996): 7–28. Also, Elizabeth Shown Mills, "Genealogy in the 'Information Age': History's New Frontier?" *National Genealogical Society Quarterly* 91 (December 2003): 260–77. Also, Elizabeth Shown Mills, "Working with Historical Evidence: Genealogical Principles and Standards," *National Genealogical Society Quarterly* 87 (September 1999): 165–84.

2. Helen F. M. Leary, "Evidence Revisited—DNA, POE, and GPS," *OnBoard: Newsletter of the Board for Certification of Genealogists* 4 (January 1998): 1–2 and 5.

3. Board for Certification of Genealogists, *The BCG Genealogical Standards Manual* (Orem, Utah: Ancestry, 2000): 1–2.

Similarly, the written explanation (element 5) incorporates the other four elements. Consequently, genealogical proof cannot be partial—a conclusion failing to demonstrate any GPS element is unproved.

The GPS's five elements can make our genealogical work both trustworthy and longstanding:

- Thorough research reduces the probabilty that newfound evidence will overturn a proved conclusion. If new evidence arises, it more likely will support or augment that conclusion than to call it into question.

- Citations describe sources supporting the conclusion and show those sources' qualities as providers of evidence. By showing the basis on which a conclusion rests, citations enable research consumers to see how trustworthy it is.

- Analysis and correlation test genealogical evidence. Analysis shows that the conclusion rests on the most-likely accurate sources available. Correlation shows that the proof reflects what combined relevant evidence shows. Together, analysis and correlation show that a conclusion is unbiased.

- Resolution of conflicting evidence ensures that all relevant evidence, not just part of it, supports the conclusion.

- A written conclusion makes the proof transparent to others. It consequently lays a foundation for future researchers to extend a family's history.

Modern technologies and genealogical proof

Twenty-first-century technology advancements have facilitated genealogical research in many ways. They have not, however, reduced our need for a standard for acceptable conclusions. Today we need the GPS even more than we did in the 1990s.

The Internet, databases, massive indexing projects, and sophisticated search tools have added new dimensions to how we locate and examine much genealogical source material. These advances have not changed how we interpret and use sources, whether digitized or not. Explaining how to use and interpret the myriad kinds of genealogical sources is beyond this book's scope, but chapter 4 provides a brief listing of printed and online resources for acquiring source-specific knowledge and skill.

Personal genealogy computer programs and online sharing of computer-generated genealogical reports bring countless newly compiled genealogies to our desktops, but their accuracy is mixed. The GPS helps us identify their useful data.

DNA testing gives family historians access to biological data via DNA records and reports. We must interpret these documents in the same way we interpret other kinds of complex sources (land records, for example).

DNA samples that do—or do not—match are genealogically significant, but without documentary data DNA reports cannot help support or disprove any conclusion of relationship or nonrelationship. The GPS is as important in contexts using DNA results as it is in contexts without them.[4]

Research and reasoning cycles

Genealogists who systematically aim for proof use five-stage research and reasoning cycles to achieve that goal:

1. *Question.* We begin with questions about a documented person's unknown relationships or other information we want to learn about that person. Chapter 2 describes this process.

2. *Gather evidence.* We examine sources that seem relevant to our research questions and note tentative answers—evidence—that information items suggest. Chapter 3 describes this process.

3. *Test hypotheses.* We determine the accuracy of evidence items by subjecting them to tests of analysis and correlation. Chapter 5 explains these tests and how to use them.

4. *Establish conclusions.* Hypotheses passing tests of accuracy become conclusions, if no evidence conflicts with the conclusion. If a conflict does exist, we must resolve it before we can assemble the evidence to establish a conclusion. Chapter 6 describes these processes.

5. *Prove.* When we explain our conclusions in writing in a way that meets the GPS's five elements our conclusions become proved. Chapter 7 explains ways to write proved genealogical conclusions.

Using the GPS

Our goal is to prove our conclusions. While we are researching, proof is just a target. By searching thoroughly and keeping track of our sources, we aim for that target. Proof is the outcome of research, not part of it. We do not achieve proof—we do not hit the target—until we complete the research, evaluate and assemble the evidence, resolve any conflicts, explain our conclusion in writing, and share it with others. Only then can we and readers of our family histories and reports assess and understand our results' accuracy.

We apply the same standard to others' genealogical research. Examining a family history in print or online, we look at the compiler's source citations to assess the research extent and likely accuracy of the sources supporting the author's conclusions. We look in the compiler's narrative for explanations of the evidence and reasoning behind the conclusions. If we find them convincing, we accept the compiler's findings as credible.

---

4. For one of many recent published examples of using DNA data with the GPS, see Warren C. Pratt, "Finding the Father of Henry Pratt of Southeastern Kentucky," *National Genealogical Society Quarterly* 100 (June 2012): 85–103.

Chapter 1 exercises

1. What is genealogy?

2. What are the GPS's five elements?

3. You have shared your family history with someone who wants you to omit all the proof statements, proof summaries, and proof arguments, including explanations of reasoning and documentation. How do you reply?

4. Why can't a genealogical conclusion be partially proved?

5. What is the first step in genealogical research?

Check your answers at the back of the book.

Chapter 2

Concepts Fundamental to the GPS

All five parts of the GPS rest on our research questions, the sources we use to investigate those questions, the information those sources provide, and our use of that information as genealogical evidence.

Research questions

Research in any field is designed to answer focused questions. Genealogy is no different. Focused genealogical questions also frame our research scope, lead us to relevant information, and help us identify evidence. They yield answers clear enough for us to show others that these answers correctly reflect the relationships, identities, and events we sought to understand.

Genealogical proof is easier to achieve and demonstrate when we plan our research to answer focused questions. These questions have two characteristics:

1. They concern a documented person.

2. They seek specific information about that person (usually a relationship or some aspect of identity or activity).

We avoid questions that are too broad or too narrow, because they are unlikely to lead to an unambiguously correct answer:

- Too-broad questions allow several correct answers.

   For example, *Who was Eleanor Medley?* could have many unrelated answers that are difficult to assess for accuracy. Better questions would be W*ho were Eleanor Medley's parents? Where did she live? What was her religion?*

- Too-narrow questions may be unanswerable with records of a place and time.

   For example, *What was Obediah Overton's exact birth date?* A better question would be *When was Obediah Overton born?* This allows a year, or a range of years, to be a correct answer.

We also avoid questions with unsupportable assumptions. For example, *What was Nellie Jourdan's real name?* assumes that a record of a single, stable legal name existed in a time when spellings varied from one record keeper to the next or that a name on a certain kind of record is more valid than a variant on another record—both rare conditions before the modern age.

Most major genealogical research questions fit one of three categories:

1. *Relationship*

   For example, *Who were the parents of A. B. Buss who lived in Jackson County, Michigan, in 1840?*

2. *Identity*

   For example, *Which Benjamin Jones paying taxes in King George County, Virginia, in the 1820s and 1830s was Watts Jones's son?*

3. *Activity*

   For example, *What service (if any) did Josiah Burton, whose children were born in Norwich, Vermont, in the 1760s, provide during the Revolutionary War?*

Supporting questions help guide genealogical research to answer the major questions of relationship, identity, and activity. Supporting questions include questions about names, dates of events, places where they occurred, and various biographical details.

> For example, *When and where was A. B. Buss born? Who were his siblings? In what tax district did each Benjamin Jones live? Who were each Benjamin's neighbors? Did Josiah Burton of Norwich, or his widow, apply for a Revolutionary War pension?*

Sources

To obtain answers to our research questions, we consult sources. Most genealogical sources are published or unpublished written material or images of such textual material. Sometimes they are artifacts, like gravestones, needlework, photographs, and scrapbooks. Genealogical sources rarely are people; instead we use records of what people have experienced, observed, and said.

Records are perhaps the most helpful genealogical sources because they were created to describe, document, memorialize, or note actions, events, observations, and utterances in which genealogists are interested. Actions, events, observations, and utterances are transitory—we cannot examine them repeatedly to ensure we interpreted them accurately, and others cannot consult them to check our work. Records—whether of DNA markers, instrument settings, oral statements, actions, or events—are much more useful because we can use them to verify our readings and interpretations. Examining DNA and hearing oral history are nearly useless activities, for example, if no one makes a record of what they saw or heard.

Source refers to an entire item, not the information or evidence within it. In other words, sources are containers, not contents. Sources include specific books, censuses, certificates, compiled and narrative genealogies, court packets, deed and will books, DNA records or reports, family Bibles, manuscript and published volumes of vital records, newspapers, religious records, websites, and many other containers of genealogically useful information.

Genealogists use facsimiles of sources as often as we use unimaged physical sources. Facsimiles include digital images (from filming, photography, or scanning), microfiche, microfilm, reprints, photocopies, and photographs. Facsimiles usually reproduce exactly what underlying physical sources show. If a facsimile shows no blurring, cropping, or evidence of alteration, we use it as if we are using the physical source from which the facsimile was imaged.

Finding aids, indexes, and search engines usually are not genealogical sources. Their purpose, like that of a book's index, is to lead us to the useful information, not to provide it. Databases are similar. If a searchable database contains images from books, files, microfilm, or photographs, those images are the sources, but the searchable database or search engine is a finding aid or index. Databases and indexes, however, may help document negative evidence and nonproductive searches, since our only alternative in these instances would be to read every word the source contains.

No kind of genealogical source is immune to error, but some sources are less error-prone than others. Land and probate records, for example, contain proportionally fewer errors than censuses.

Categories of genealogical sources

Genealogical sources and their facsimiles can be divided into two broad types:[1]

- *Authored works*—like a case study, family genealogy, or military history—present a researcher's or writer's conclusions, interpretations, or thoughts, often based on information from many prior sources.

- *Records* note, describe, or document an action, event, observation, or utterance.

Records may be further divided into either original or derivative:

- *Original records* are written reports of an action, event, or observation, often (but not always) made at the time of the event or soon after. Original records are not based on prior records.

---

1. The author thanks Elizabeth Shown Mills, CG, CGL, FASG, FNGS, for articulating this distinction. See Elizabeth Shown Mills, "QuickLesson 10: Original Records, Image Copies, and Derivatives," *Evidence Explained: Historical Analysis, Citation and Source Usage* (https://www.evidenceexplained.com/content/quicklesson-10-original-records-image-copies-and-derivatives : viewed 1 August 2012), footnote 1.

- *Derivative records* are created from prior records by (*1*) transcribing a prior record or part of it by hand, keyboard, or optical-character-recognition, speech-to-text, or other technology, (*2*) abstracting information from it, (*3*) translating it from one language to another, or (*4*) reproducing it with alterations.

Authored work, original record, and *derivative record* are permanent attributes of sources. Circumstances, research questions and answers, and other variables will not change an authored work into a record or vice versa, and they will not change an original record into a derivative record or vice versa. For example, a death certificate created by copying information from a death register onto a form always will be a derivative record.

Importance of source distinctions

The authored/original/derivative-source distinction helps our research in three important ways:

- *It alerts us to sources that may be more error prone than others.* The process of creating an authored work or derivative record may introduce errors of reading, writing, and interpretation that do not appear in the original record.

- *It causes us to pursue originals.* Because we want to use the most accurate sources available, when we recognize a source is authored, we check the author's sources, especially if the work had not been vetted or subjected to fact checking. If a record is derivative, we seek the original record on which it is based. We are more likely to prove conclusions with original records than with authored works or derivative records.

- *It strengthens our conclusions' credibility.* If we do not base our conclusions on the least error-prone sources available, our work's accuracy and usefulness (and our credibility as genealogists) suffer. We base conclusions on a derivative record only when the original record no longer exists or is inaccessible. We base conclusions on an authored work only when we are certain that experts vetted the work and checked its sources.

Information

Information refers to a source's surface content, including written or oral statements. Information may arise from experience, fabrication, hearsay, intuition, observation, reading, research, or some other means. Information items may be statements about people, groups, and events. They also may be just an age, date, land description, location, military rank, monetary amount, name, occupation, role, or other detail. Information includes physical appearance, like handwriting characteristics or details in a photograph. Information does not refer to our interpretations of what these statements, details, and physical characteristics mean. It refers only to what we see or hear.

Informants

Information usually comes from an informant—someone who provided information of interest. Informants report events they witnessed. They also retell information they heard. Informants sometimes create information, perhaps inferring it from their experiences or sources or simply by inventing it.

Sources may identify informants. The person signing a record or swearing to its accuracy often is the informant. On the other hand, record keepers recording information that others tell them—census takers, court clerks, interviewers, and oral historians, for example—usually are not informants. Pre-1940 federal-census informants usually are unknown, and court-record informants often are a judge or witness whose statements the clerk records. Sometimes an informant also is the recorder—for example, an adolescent writing a diary of her observations and experiences, a religious official recording a marriage or burial he performed, or a widow writing her own affidavit or will.

When a source doesn't identify its informant, we sometimes can infer the informant's identity. In other cases, such inference is not possible and the informant remains unknown.

Categories of genealogical information

If—and only if—we can identify a statement's informant, we can classify the information item:

1. *Primary information* is that reported by an eyewitness. Primary information often was recorded soon after the event, but it may be reported or recorded years or decades later.

   For example, a pension applicant's statement about his military service or an aged interviewee's account of her childhood experiences may be primary information.

2. *Secondary information* is reported by someone who obtained it from someone else. It is hearsay. Secondary information begins as primary information. It becomes secondary when someone who did not witness an event or relationship reports it.

   For example, an interviewee describing her grandparents' childhood immigration experiences reports secondary information—the interviewee did not witness or experience the immigration; her report is hearsay.

If we cannot identify a statement's informant or we cannot determine how an identified informant obtained information, we can classify the information item only one way:

> 3. *Indeterminable.*

Sources usually contain many information items, which may come from several informants, perhaps including unknown informants. In these cases we must separately assess each item relevant to our research question. One source may include information items that are primary, others that are secondary, and still others that have an unknown origin. For example, a physician's statement on a death certificate about a cause of death, and a sexton's statement about the burial, may be primary information, but the designated informant's statement about the deceased person's birth and parents may be secondary information.

Just as sources may contain primary, secondary, and indeterminable information, one informant may provide all three kinds of information. A bride's report of her marriage date, for example, is primary information, but her report of her birth date is secondary information. She knows the marriage date because she witnessed the marriage and remembers it; she knows the birth date because someone told her.

Primary, secondary, and *indeterminable* are permanent attributes of information. Circumstances, research questions and answers, and other variables will not change an eyewitness's description into hearsay and vice versa.

Importance of information distinctions

Like the authored/original/derivative-source distinction, the primary/secondary/indeterminable-information distinction helps our research in three important ways:

- *It alerts us to information items that may be more error prone than others.* Retelling introduces exaggerations, omissions, and inventions. Compared to eyewitness accounts, retellings are more vulnerable to mishearing, misinterpreting, and misremembering. Secondary information items, therefore, are more error-prone than primary information items.

- *It causes us to pursue primary information.* Because we want to use the most accurate sources available, when we recognize that a relevant information item is secondary or has an unknown informant, we seek eyewitness reports.

- *It strengthens our conclusions' credibility.* If we do not base our conclusions on the least error-prone sources available, our work's accuracy suffers. We base conclusions on information that is secondary or has unknown origin only when corresponding primary information is unfindable.

Relationship of sources and information

The concepts of *source* (container) and *information* (content) are distinct and do not affect each other. Similar contents can be found in different kinds of containers, and one kind of container can hold different kinds of contents.

Inexperienced genealogists sometimes equate derivative records with secondary information, but they confuse the container with its contents:

- An original record may contain primary, secondary, or indeterminable information or any combination of the three.

   For example, a burial record (original record) may include the burial date and place (information reported by the priest who witnessed the burial—therefore, primary information) and the deceased person's birth data and parentage (information told to the priest—therefore, secondary information).

- A derivative record may contain primary, secondary, or indeterminable information or any combination of the three.

   For example, an online transcription of a recorded interview (derivative source) may include the interviewee's identification of her parents (primary information) and her descent from a Revolutionary War soldier (secondary information).

- Creating a derivative record from an original record does not change its primary information to secondary.

   For example, compiling a book of abstracts (derivative record) from a will book (original record) does not change the testators' identifications of their children from primary information to secondary information. The abstracting process affects the entire source, not selected information items. Consequently the authored/original/derivative-*source* distinction, not the primary/secondary/indeterminable-*information* distinction, applies.

- An authored work amalgamating others' information might seem to be derivative—the author used many sources—but authored works technically are not derivative. Authors typically combine information from numerous sources and use the combination to create their own conclusions, descriptions, ideas, and interpretations. These may exist nowhere except in the authored work. Authored works, even those containing no eyewitness information, usually are new creations.

Evidence

Evidence items are genealogical proof's building blocks. We gather evidence to learn about events, identities, and relationships that we cannot observe directly. An information item becomes evidence when we consider its implications for what an unobservable event, identity, or relationship might have been. Consequently, evidence is intangible. Sources and information can be seen, touched, and heard, but evidence exists in our minds.

Evidence items suggest answers to research questions. As tentative answers, evidence items do not exist in a question's absence. Although an evidence item suggests an answer, that answer is not a conclusion—proved conclusions rest on the "sum" of multiple evidence items that have passed tests of accuracy, never on just one building block.

Evidence can be right or wrong, complete or partial, and specific or vague. We can't be certain a tentative answer is correct until we have completed research and reasoning processes (including testing the evidence), and proving the conclusions that aggregated evidence items indicate.

As our research progresses we consider many possibilities. Some may compete or conflict—for example, we may have evidence that John's mother was Mary Smith and that she was Sylvia Jones. We eventually will assess these possibilities and discard or accept one or both of them. When we consider many alternative possibilities during our research's evidence-gathering phase, however, we increase our opportunities to develop a provable conclusion.

Categories of genealogical evidence

We use information items as evidence directly, indirectly, or negatively:

- *Direct evidence* is an information item that answers a research question all by itself. When we consider the possibility that an information item describes what actually occurred we are using that information item as direct evidence.

  > For example, if the question is *What was the maiden name of the wife of Obediah Overton who lived in Culpeper County, Virginia, in 1806?* and Obediah's marriage record says he married "Ellender Crow," the marriage record provides direct evidence that Obediah's wife's first name was Ellender.

- *Indirect evidence* is a set of two or more information items that suggest an answer to a research question only when they are combined.

  > For example, James Crow's orphan's choosing the above Obediah to be her guardian suggests, in view of Obediah's marriage record, the possibility that Obediah's wife Ellender was James Crow's widow. The guardianship record's evidence is indirect because it does not suggest that answer all by itself—the evidence from Obediah and Ellender's marriage record also must be considered. Tax records and a deed, showing that Obediah and Ellender sold land on which James Crow had paid taxes, bring further evidence indirectly answering the question about Obediah's wife's identity. Their evidence suggests, or is consistent with, the answer that Ellender was James's widow. Because none of those sources state that relationship, this evidence is indirect. Because evidence is not

proof, the indirect evidence suggesting that Ellender was James Crow's widow remains tentative until all GPS elements are met.

- *Negative evidence* is the absence of information that answers a research question.

  For example, a county's pre-1820 tax lists in which a research subject is not listed may provide evidence that the research subject was a minor, too old to pay taxes, deceased, or living elsewhere.

Combining information from different sources does not make evidence indirect. All genealogical conclusions rest on aggregated evidence, and the aggregation may consist of direct evidence, indirect evidence, negative evidence, or a combination.

> Suppose, for example, the question is *When was James Wright who died in Columbia County, Georgia, in 1862 born?* The 1850 census shows he was age 49, and the 1860 census says 60. Each census answers the question directly—the 1850 answer is 1800–1801, and the 1860 answer is 1799–1800. We might combine those answers to deduce that James was born in 1800, but each census gives an answer directly. This differs from the Obediah Overton indirect-evidence example, in which the guardianship selection, tax records, and deed do not answer the question alone. In that case, any answer is apparent only when we consider the evidence from those sources together.

While direct evidence usually is what a source says, calculation based on information from one source does not make the evidence indirect.

> Suppose our question is *When was Abigail Burton who died in Norwich, Vermont, in 1836 born?* and her gravestone says she died on 30 December 1836 at age 20 years, 6 months, and 5 days. Although we calculate her birth date as 25 June 1816, the gravestone's evidence is direct because we did not combine its information about Abigail's age at death with other information—the gravestone gives that answer all by itself.

Importance of evidence distinctions

Direct evidence is obvious and easy to use. Believing surface information to be true—using it directly—requires little analysis, evaluation, synthesis, or other critical thinking skills. Most genealogists understand and use direct evidence, though they might not use the term or have considered the concept.

Indirect and negative evidence items, in contrast, are buried. They must be detected, and this detection requires higher-order thinking skills, like deductive and inductive reasoning. Genealogists who are not attuned to indirect and negative evidence will miss it, even where it is ubiquitous. The direct/indirect/negative-evidence distinction reminds us to attend to details and possibilities we might otherwise miss.

Understanding the differences between direct, indirect, and negative evidence helps us see evidence that is easy to overlook, including implied answers that prove to be correct despite what surface information says. This understanding also helps us establish conclusions in the absence of any source stating the answer we seek—a common scenario. Indirect and negative evidence items, therefore, help us solve complex problems and break through genealogical brick walls.

Some genealogists believe they cannot establish proof without direct evidence. This belief reflects a misunderstanding. The Genealogical Proof Standard does not require direct evidence. Proof rests on the sum of evidence—any kind of evidence—arising from thorough research. Articles in the *National Genealogical Society Quarterly* and comparable journals regularly provide examples of proof achieved without direct evidence.

Relationship of sources and information to evidence

Genealogical sources, information, and evidence are related in that sources contain information, and we use information items as evidence. Evidence, however, differs from sources and information in three fundamental ways:

- *We use the authored/original/derivative-source and primary/secondary/indeterminable-information distinctions to assess vulnerabilities to error* and guide us to the most likely accurate sources and information. The direct/indirect/negative-evidence distinction, however, does not indicate vulnerability to error. Using evidence indirectly or negatively introduces no more error than using it directly. Evidence errors vary with our reasoning skills, not with the material we use.

- *Sources and information are tangibles, but evidence is not.* We can touch a source. An information item is what a source says on its surface—we can see or hear it. An evidence item, however, is what the information item means to us in the context of our research question. Evidence is our interpretation of the information a source provides. It exists only in our minds.

- *Source and information categories are stable, but evidence categories are not.* Source and information categories do not vary as research questions, answers, and circumstances change. In contrast, evidence categories do vary with our research question and its answer.

  Suppose, for example, our research question is *Where did John Kinzer live?* and a 1 June 1810 deed refers to grantor John Kinzer "of Culpeper County." Thus, the record gives us direct evidence of John's residence by stating it.

  Suppose, on the other hand, our research question is *When was John Kinzer born?* For this question, combining the deed's date with the common-law requirement that grantors be at least age twenty-one gives the answer *before 1 June 1790.* That evidence is indirect because the law does not mention John and the deed does not state his age; only together do they provide an answer.

Chapter 2 exercises

1. Read the article in appendix A and identify the major question the research was designed to answer.

2. List two other questions in the same article that the reported research answers.

3. Read the article in appendix B and identify the major question or questions the research was designed to answer.

4. List two other questions in the same article that the reported research answers.

5. Using this chapter's criteria for effective research questions (pages 7–8), write three relationship research questions like the example on page 8, but for research you plan to undertake.

6. Using this chapter's criteria for effective research questions, write one identity research question like the example on page 8, but for research you plan to undertake.

7. Using this chapter's criteria for effective research questions, write one activity research question like the example on page 8, but for research you plan to undertake.

8. List four authored works (not derivative records) cited in the articles in appendixes A and B.

9. List four original records cited in the article in appendix A.

10. List four derivative records cited in the article in appendix A.

11. Explain why you would prefer an original record containing primary information over a derivative record containing secondary information.

12. Suppose you find an entry of interest in "California Birth Index, 1905–1995," on *Ancestry.com* (http://search.ancestry.com/search/db.aspx?dbid =5247&enc=1). What should be your next step?

13. Follow the model in the table and list elements of three additional primary information items and three secondary information items with identified informants in the article in appendix B.

INFORMATION ITEM	TYPE	SOURCE	INFORMANT
Ida's husband was a carpenter	*primary*	*testimony in circuit court case file (note 12)*	*Calista J. Tucker, Ida's mother*

14. In the following table list three additional information items from the article in appendix A that the author uses as direct evidence. Follow the example to fill in the following for each item: its source, the question the evidence answers, and the answer it gives.

INFORMATION ITEM	SOURCE	QUESTION	ANSWER
Naming "Alpherd" and Lewis among "all my children"	*Will Book A:106–7*	*Who were Philip's children?*	*"Alpherd," Lewis, and others unnamed*

15. In the table below, list three additional sets of information items from the article in appendix A that the author uses together as indirect evidence. Follow the example to fill in the following for each set of items: its source or sources, the question the evidence answers, and the answer it gives.

INFORMATION ITEMS	SOURCES	QUESTION	ANSWER
Philip Pritchett paid Kentucky taxes in 1797; as a minor he sued in Fauquier County in 1783 with "next friend" Lewis Pritchett. The Kentucky Philip was over age 45 in 1810, he had a son Lewis, and his executor came from Fauquier County.	*The sources cited in appendix A, notes 4 and 6–8*	*Was the adult Philip Pritchett in Kentucky the minor in the Virginia lawsuit?*	*Yes*

16. In the table below, list two or more additional absence-of-information items from the article in appendix A that the author uses as negative evidence. Follow the example to fill in the following for each information item you list: its source, the question that the evidence answers, and the answer it gives.

ABSENCE-OF-INFORMATION ITEM	SOURCE	QUESTION	ANSWER
Philip did not pay taxes in Fauquier County	*Tax lists (note 13)*	*Did Philip live in Fauquier County?*	*No*

17. Explain why one of your answers to question 15 is an example of indirect evidence and not direct evidence.

18. Explain why one of your answers to question 16 is an example of negative evidence and not direct evidence.

Check your answers at the back of the book.

Chapter 3

GPS Element 1: Thorough Research[1]

An appropriate research scope enhances our ability to recognize erroneous information, test hypotheses, and assemble enough evidence to support and prove a valid conclusion.

The GPS's first element, a "reasonably exhaustive search," is designed to ensure our genealogical conclusions do not totter on incomplete research or inaccurate evidence. We want to use the most authoritative sources possible, and we do not want to bypass any source that might help answer our research question. Thorough research will minimize the possibility that overlooked evidence will overturn a conclusion we thought we had proved. An appropriate research scope also enhances our ability to recognize erroneous information, test hypotheses, and assemble enough evidence to establish a valid conclusion. If our research were to bypass known likely-helpful sources, people using our results would distrust them, even if our results were correct.

What "reasonably exhaustive" means

Numerous, varied, and widespread materials offer nearly infinite possibilities for genealogical information. An exhaustive search would require examining them all, but consulting a near-infinite number of sources is impossible. If, however, we focus on specific questions and examine the sources likely to help answer those questions, our research extent will be manageable.

Only a small fraction of the near-infinite number of sources is likely to offer relevant evidence answering a focused research question. Six criteria help us temper the exhaustive search to make it reasonable. Those criteria guide our selection of a relevant subset of sources to examine:

1. *At least two independently-created evidence items in agreement.* One item rarely suffices for proof, because sources contain errors that only comparisons expose. Cases where direct evidence conflicts or is absent usually require more evidence than other cases. Directly, indirectly,

---

1. This chapter draws heavily from Thomas W. Jones, How Much Searching is 'Reasonably Exhaustive'?" *Association of Professional Genealogists Quarterly* 25 (March 2010): 25–33.

negatively, or in combination, the minimum of two evidence items should provide the same answer to our research question. That answer must come from independent sources or informants—one must not be based on another. Independent items corroborate each other, but items sharing the same origin or informant—a gravestone's birth date copied from a family Bible, for example—just duplicate each other. Using the same evidence item twice (or more times) does not increase its accuracy or add any credibility to a conclusion.

2. *All sources competent genealogists would examine.* These include (*a*) sources likely to answer our research question and (*b*) sources that might offer competing answers. Genealogical research rarely is complete without census, land, probate, and vital records, but each research question's specifics and its geographic and chronological setting suggest unique combinations of relevant sources. Generic checklists rarely offer guidance beyond a superficial level, requiring us to rely on research guides, education, and experience to identify sources with potential to answer a research question. The sources we consider may extend beyond the obvious. For example, home sources and birth and baptismal records name parents with a relatively low error rate, but our research should include sources likely to confirm or challenge one source's evidence of parentage and reduce the likelihood of error. Confirmation might come, for example, from censuses, marriage or death records, obituaries, pension files, or records of inheritance, land transfers, and other court actions. See table 1 for guides to identifying the availability of relevant sources.

3. *Some primary information.* Hearsay often provides useful details, but proof based only on secondary information is questionable because hearsay is more vulnerable to error than eyewitness reports. Valid conclusions may include hearsay, but at least one supporting direct, indirect, or negative evidence item must be based on eyewitness information.

4. *Some original records.* Authored works and derivative records may provide useful information, but proof based only on authored works and derivative records is questionable because they are more vulnerable to error than original records. The sum of evidence supporting genealogical proof may include evidence from authored works and derivative records, but at least one supporting direct, indirect, or negative evidence item should come from an original record.

5. *Relevant authored works, derivative records, and secondary information replaced by findable corresponding originals and primary information.* Convenience may tempt us to base proof on authored works, derivative records, or secondary information items that are more easily accessible than better sources and information. If the original of a potentially useful authored work or derivative record is findable, or if the primary informant's record can be located, we enhance our conclusion's credibility by using the more likely accurate and complete source and information, despite extra effort or expense. We

Table 1

Suggestions for Identifying Sources to Answer Genealogical Questions

- Study research guides for relevant geographic areas:
  - National Genealogical Society's *Research in the States* series (See http://www.ngsgenealogy.org/cs/ngs_special_publications.)
  - Other published print and online guides to genealogical research in specific states, cities, and regions

- Visit archives, courthouses, historical societies, libraries, town halls, and other repositories in areas related to specific research questions and consult with knowledgeable staff members.

- Consult catalogs of large genealogy libraries and archives, including:
  - Family History Library (http://familysearch.org/eng/Library/FHLC/frameset.asp)
  - National Society Daughters of the American Revolution (http://dar.org/library/onlinlin.cfm)
  - New England Historic Genealogical Society (http://library.nehgs.org)

- Search *WorldCat* (http://www.worldcat.org) for relevant library and historical society book and manuscript holdings. (*WorldCat* includes many libraries with important genealogy collections, including the Allen County Public Library, Library of Congress, Mid-Continent Public Library, and Saint Louis County Library.)

- Search the *National Union Catalog of Manuscript Collections* (NUCMC) in print and online for unpublished materials in archives, historical societies, and manuscript collections.

- Examine online guides to genealogical records, including:
  - *Cyndi's List* (http://cyndislist.com/)
  - FamilySearch's *Research Wiki* (https://familysearch.org/learn/wiki/en/Main_Page)
  - *Linkpendium* (http://www.linkpendium.com/)

- Use the *Periodical Source Index* (PERSI) to locate articles relevant to specific research questions.

- Study documented articles and compiled genealogies of families in relevant areas, even when the families seem to be of no interest, to learn about the sources their authors used.

base proof on more-error-prone sources and information only when less-error-prone sources and information do not exist and we have no better option.

6. *All findable sources that relevant sources and indexes suggest.* When a source, database, or index suggests a source is relevant to our search—a death certificate indicated by a death index, for example, or court minutes or a case file implied by a deed's wording—we try to locate the source. If it is available, we examine it. We are not satisfied with references to sources, because they usually provide fewer, if not less-accurate, information items than the source itself.

Planning thorough research

We often begin genealogical research with a family's oral history or previous research. Beyond that starting point, possibilities for expanding the search include local, state, regional, or national cemetery, census, courthouse, land, migration, military, newspaper, pension, religious, tax, town-hall, and vital records—whether or not available on microfilm—and websites offering images of the above. We may examine family papers and unique manuscripts at various kinds of archives, historical societies, libraries, and other repositories; original and derivative published works; and online and offline electronic resources. We also might obtain reports of various kinds of DNA tests.

Exactly what we examine depends on our research questions, the hypotheses we need to test, what is available for the time and place, our knowledge and expertise, and the six criteria discussed above. Difficult cases require broad searches covering sources relevant to several families, surnames, and communities over several generations. Narrow searches may suffice for simple, straightforward cases. Convenience, expertise, financing, location, or practical concerns may limit our plan's scope and jeopardize our ability to prove a conclusion. Ideally, however, four goals guide our selection of materials to examine:

1. *Identifying material that may be relevant to our research question or hypothesis.* For this purpose research often begins with databases, finding aids, holdings inventories, indexes, library catalogs, research guides, search engines, and similar materials. As our research progresses, sources may indicate other sources to examine—for example, a real-estate value on a census suggests deed and land-tax records are relevant. We may find it helpful to cite finding aids in our works in progress, but rarely do we use them to document our finished proof statements, summaries, and arguments. There, we cite the supporting sources that they led us to.

2. *Obtaining information and evidence to help answer our research question.* The exact sources vary as described above.

3. *Using accurate sources.* Our research should give priority to likely-accurate records—those containing eyewitness or participant information recorded soon after the reported events. In ideal situations impartial officials questioned the informant, made the record, tried to verify its accuracy, and kept it free from harm.

4. *Attempting to reject hypotheses.* We cannot confirm a research hypothesis if we cannot eliminate hypotheses competing with it. Negative evidence often serves this purpose in genealogy—the absence of evidence that John Doe married anyone other than Jane Roe rules out hypotheses of wives besides Jane. It verifies the Doe-Roe marriage record and supports a conclusion that the mother of all John's children was Jane Roe. Negative evidence is credible only when the research covers all sources likely to contain information competing with our working hypothesis. For example, if both civil and religious marriage records survive for John Doe's time and place, searching for him in one but not the other could undermine our conclusion.

Before examining a source we usually will not know its specific contents. This makes choices of materials to examine tentative. We do not overplan, because difficult-to-foresee changes in direction waste effort invested in an extensive research plan. We begin with a person or family, a location, a time frame, and one or more focused research questions. As information accumulates it may lead to people, places, and sources not previously considered, and new questions may emerge. Our subset of nearly infinite sources may grow and grow.

The Genealogical Proof Standard, although not intended to guide research planning, offers a yardstick for measuring completed research's credibility. Consequently, "reasonably exhaustive" applies to end products, not plans. Planning research is good practice, but a plan, no matter how extensive, might not lead to proof.

When applied to research planning and execution, the question *How extensive is "reasonable"?* is unanswerable. Our plan's ultimate goal may be proof, but research extent typically is unknown before we complete the project. If our evidence is insufficient for proof, our only options are to continue searching or quit. Deciding to quit or continue searching because our research has been insufficiently productive is different from deciding to stop searching because our accumulated evidence is sufficient for proof. "Reasonably exhaustive" applies only to the latter decision.

When planning research for medium and large projects, we are best advised to start by restricting them to likely-informative sources, rather than designing a comprehensive search at the outset. As research progresses, however, additions to the plan might lead to a result that could be judged "reasonably exhaustive."

Executing thorough research

The genealogical research process involves a series of activities:

1. We begin by identifying sources likely to contain information relevant to our research questions and locating those sources. They typically are available in several places and media. Useful sources include digitized text and images on the Internet and elsewhere, print and microfilmed material at libraries and FamilySearch centers, and unique manuscripts and artifacts in archives, cemeteries, churches, courthouses, family homes, historical societies, town halls, and other repositories. Search engines, finding aids, and genealogical research guides like those mentioned in table 1 may lead us to many of these sources.

2. We examine each source or selected portions, cite it, and note exactly what we examined, what we were looking for, and what we found. If we find information that seems relevant to our research questions, we write notes about it or transcribe or abstract selected items or portions of items. We also may create digital images, photocopies, and printouts. If the source fails to provide information that seems relevant to our research, we note—as specifically as we can—what we did not find.

3. Based on information we did and did not find in the sources we examined, we identify additional sources and repeat step 2.

4. We repeat steps 2 and 3 until we believe we have an answer to our research question that will meet the GPS's criterion for thorough research.

Genealogical searches progress along a continuum ranging from one source to a near-infinite number. Exhaustive searches approach infinity, but reasonable searches stop well short of that point. Where—or if—we stop depends on what we have and have not found. We stop when we believe we have accumulated sufficient evidence to meet the six criteria discussed above, under *What "reasonably exhaustive" means.* If we do not believe we have enough evidence, our only options are to give up or to continue searching.

Demonstrating research extent

Per the GPS's second element, genealogical proof statements, summaries, and arguments include source citations. Among the most important of their several purposes, these citations reveal our research extent. By examining citations supporting a conclusion, readers can see whether or not our research was thorough enough to prove the conclusion. We similarly can examine others' citations to determine the adequacy of their research scope. These assessments include six questions based on the criteria described above for a reasonably exhaustive search:

1. Do our supporting citations document at least two evidence items from independent sources and informants in agreement?

2. Do those citations reference all sources competent genealogists would examine to prove an answer to our research question?

3. Does any supporting citation document primary information?

4. Does any supporting citation document an original source?

5. Did we cite authored works and derivative records only to document unproductive searches providing negative evidence or only when a corresponding original record does not survive? Did we cite sources providing secondary or indeterminable information only when sources providing corresponding primary information do not survive?

6. Do our citations reference all useful findable sources that relevant sources and indexes suggest?

Chapter 3 exercises

1. The research reported in appendix A addresses the research question *When was Philip Pritchett born?* and the article gives the answer *about 1763*. (See the article's page 38, first paragraph under "Conclusion.") How does the conclusion *Philip Pritchett was born about 1763* meet the six criteria for a reasonably exhaustive search? To answer this question, give specific examples from the article and its documentation for each of the following criteria:

   a. At least two independent evidence items in agreement

   b. All sources competent genealogists would examine

   c. Some primary information

     d.   Some original records

     e.   Relevant authored works, derivative records, and secondary information replaced by findable corresponding original records and primary information

     f.   All findable sources suggested by relevant sources and indexes

2. After the research reported in appendix B was published, a student discovered that the 1850 U.S. census of Mercer County, Ohio, includes the household of "Jas McLean," 23, apparent wife Phebe, 22, child Sarah, 5, and no one else. They lived near the parents and brother of Phebe (Wright) McLain. This finding requires reconsidering the article's answer to the question *When was James and Phebe's son David born?* (summarized on the article's page 119, paragraph 2). The new evidence (negative evidence, since David is not enumerated) eliminates the three sources giving evidence of his pre-1850 birth, leaving the new finding and other sources supporting the answer *between 1850 and 1854*. How does this new conclusion meet the six criteria for a reasonably exhaustive search? To answer this question, give specific examples from the article, its documentation, and the new finding for each of the following criteria:

a.   At least two evidence items in agreement

b.   All sources competent genealogists would examine

c.   Some primary information

d.   Some original records

e.   Relevant authored works, derivative records, and secondary information replaced by findable corresponding originals and primary information

f.   All findable sources suggested by relevant sources and indexes

3. Suppose you are researching Mary L. Jones, who appears in the Silas Jones and Sarah E. Jones household in the 1860 U.S. census of Hamilton County, Illinois. Your research question is *Who were Mary's parents?* Using the Family History Library catalog (https://www.familysearch .org/#form=catalog) and any other resources you wish, list finding aids and sources you might use to pursue answers to your research question. Single out at least two original records likely to provide primary information about Mary's parentage.

Check your answers at the back of the book.

Chapter 4

GPS Element 2: Source Citations

If we invent citation formats, use citation styles from nongenealogical disciplines, omit important citation elements, or apply formats that do not match our sources, communication breaks down and we undermine our attempt to prove a conclusion.

Genealogical source citations fulfill several critical purposes, but their most important use is to support genealogical proof statements, summaries, and arguments. Citations show that research scope was "reasonably exhaustive." Our citations' components and formats—sometimes along with narrative discussion—should show that our conclusions rest on the least error-prone sources available. Our citations also document our findings and explanations.

Citation components

Complete and accurate genealogical citations communicate. They introduce no confusion about our sources. Our citations tell readers exactly what we used. They indicate reliability of our sources and their information items as providers of genealogical evidence. Thoroughly understanding a source is prerequisite to citing it. If we do not understand the source's purpose, history, and context, we will not be able to communicate clearly its important features. Table 2 lists several guides to American genealogical sources that will help develop the knowledge needed to cite them clearly.

For communication to be clear our citations must use standard formats containing standard components. If we invent citation formats, use citation styles from nongenealogical disciplines, omit important citation elements, or apply formats that do not match our sources, communication breaks down and we undermine our attempt to prove a conclusion.

Five questions that citations answer

Standard genealogical citations answer five questions:

1. *Who?* The first element of most citations identifies the source's author, creator, or informant. If this entity is unknown or is the same as the

source's title or publisher (if any), we omit the *Who?* field. This element does not identify officials creating records as part of their employment, like town or county clerks, census enumerators, and religious officials. Creators of government and religious records are civil and religious bodies, like towns, counties, probate districts, churches, parishes, and synagogues.

2. *What?* The second element of most citations is a source title. If the source bears an English-language title, we capitalize it headline style. We italicize titles of published sources (like books, journals, newspapers, and websites). If we cite the title of a part of a published source, the part's title precedes the source's title. We place the part's title between quotation marks, capitalize it headline style, and do not italicize it. We also place formal titles of parts of unpublished authored works between quotation marks without italicizing. We place unpublished-record titles between quotation marks only when the title is needed to ensure the source's proper identification. If an unpublished source bears no title, we write a description capitalized sentence style (for example: *unattributed family group sheet* or *gravestone of Jane Roe*). If the nature of a source or part of a source is not evident from its title or the citation format, we add descriptive words after the title (for example: *database, digital image, typescript,* or *filled-in form*).

Table 2

Selected Guides Describing American Genealogical Sources

Note: See this book's "Reference and Source List" for descriptions of the guides.

Eakle, Arlene, and Johni Cerny. *The Source: A Guidebook of American Genealogy*. Salt Lake City: Ancestry, 1984 [best used with the third edition, cited under Szucs].

Eales, Anne Bruner, and Robert M. Kvasnicka. *Guide to Genealogical Research in the National Archives of the United States*, 3rd ed. Washington, D.C.: National Archives and Records Administration, 2000.

FamilySearch. *Research Wiki*. https://familysearch.org/learn/wiki/en/Main_Page : 2012.

Greenwood, Val D. *The Researcher's Guide to American Genealogy*, 3rd ed. Baltimore: Genealogical Publishing Company, 2000.

Mills, Elizabeth Shown. *Evidence Explained: Citing History Sources from Artifacts to Cyberspace*. Baltimore: Genealogical Publishing Company, 2009.

Rubincam, Milton, ed. *Genealogical Research: Methods and Sources*, vol. 1, 2nd ed. Washington D.C.: American Society of Genealogists, 1980.

"Skillbuilding." *Board for Certification of Genealogists*. http://www.bcgcertification.org/skillbuilders/index.html : 2012.

Stevenson, Noel C. *Genealogical Evidence: A Guide to the Standard of Proof Relating to Pedigrees, Ancestry, Heirship, and Family History*. Laguna Hills, Calif.: Aegean Park, 1979.

Szucs, Loretto Dennis, and Sandra Hargreaves Luebking. *The Source: A Guidebook to American Genealogy*, 3rd ed. Provo, Utah: Ancestry, 2006.

3. *When?* A year signifies when a book, CD-ROM, or microfilm was published. We add the month or season for journals and magazines, the exact issue date for newspapers, and the complete download date for online material. We use exact dates also for unpublished sources — the source's recordation date, the date of the event the citation documents, or both. If we can estimate a date for an undated source, we show it (for example: *likely in the 1950s* or *1812–19*). We use the word *undated* or abbreviation *n.d.* (for *no date*) when a source does not bear a date and we cannot estimate it.

4. *Where <u>in</u> the source?* Citations to printed sources provide the numbers of the volume (if applicable) and page; they usually do not mention the item of interest. Citations to unpublished sources do, however, identify items of interest (for example, *Smith-Jones marriage* or *Doe to Roe* deed), along with page or folio and volume numbers, if applicable. Citations to bound sources without page or folio numbers say *unpaginated* or identify the material's arrangement (for example, *alphabetical by groom's surname* or *chronologically arranged*).

5. *Where <u>is</u> the source?* Because unpublished sources are unique, their citations include their location — typically an agency or office with its city and state. These citations also may include location within the repository — name, number, or both of the item, file, container, series, collection, record group, and the like. The sequence may begin with the item of interest and proceed level by level to the state, or follow another sequence if the elements are clear. By definition, published sources are widely available. Consequently, their citations mention publication details, not the place we used the published source. Publication details vary with the type of source — city, state, and publisher for books, CD-ROMs, and microfilm publications; city and state for newspapers; and URL for online sources. Citations to journals and magazines omit their locations and those of their publishers.

For analysis of who-what-when-where-where elements in sample citations of published and unpublished sources, see figures 1 and 2. Footnotes in the articles in appendixes A and B contain in-context examples of genealogical citations.

Citing sources as we consult them helps us analyze them — GPS element 3. We cannot construct an adequate citation to a source if we do not understand what it is — if we cannot correctly and clearly answer the above five questions about it. Answers to those questions often show whether the cited source is an authored work or an original or derivative record and whether the relevant information item — a cited "item of interest" — is primary, secondary, or indeterminable.

Similarly, citations in finished genealogical products show consumers whether or not our conclusions and claims of proof rest on likely accurate sources. If a citation leaves a question about a source's qualities as a provider of genealogical evidence, we can add information to the reference note, as a sentence following the citation, or in our narrative text.

Figure 1

Who-What-When-Where-Where Elements in Four Citations to Published Sources

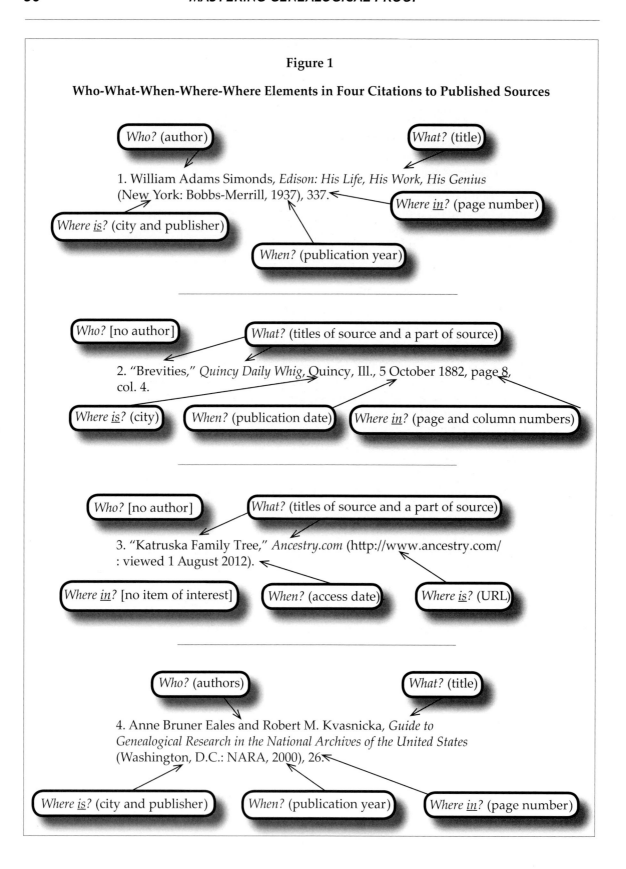

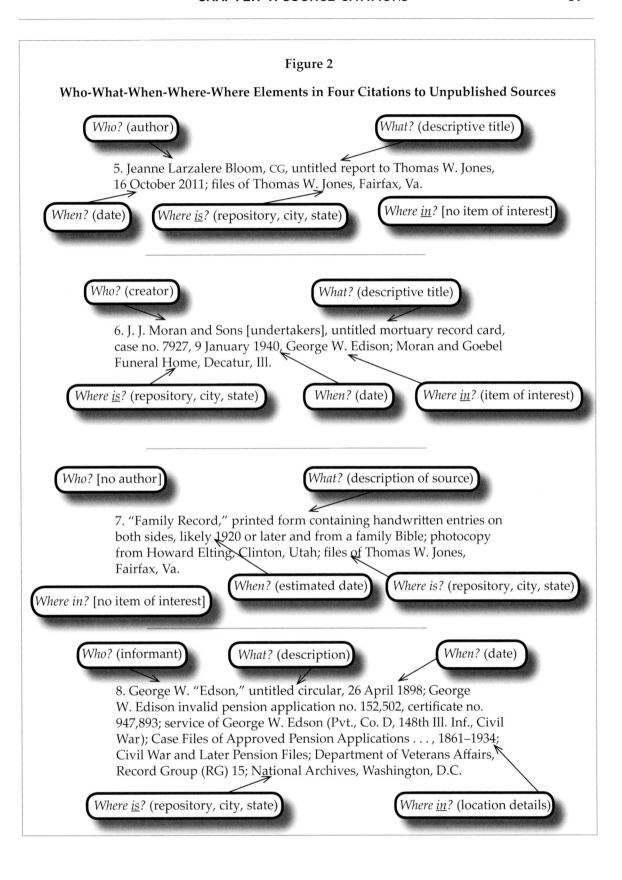

Figure 2

Who-What-When-Where-Where Elements in Four Citations to Unpublished Sources

Who? (author)

What? (descriptive title)

5. Jeanne Larzalere Bloom, CG, untitled report to Thomas W. Jones, 16 October 2011; files of Thomas W. Jones, Fairfax, Va.

When? (date)

Where is? (repository, city, state)

Where in? [no item of interest]

Who? (creator)

What? (descriptive title)

6. J. J. Moran and Sons [undertakers], untitled mortuary record card, case no. 7927, 9 January 1940, George W. Edison; Moran and Goebel Funeral Home, Decatur, Ill.

Where is? (repository, city, state)

When? (date)

Where in? (item of interest)

Who? [no author]

What? (description of source)

7. "Family Record," printed form containing handwritten entries on both sides, likely 1920 or later and from a family Bible; photocopy from Howard Elting, Clinton, Utah; files of Thomas W. Jones, Fairfax, Va.

Where in? [no item of interest]

When? (estimated date)

Where is? (repository, city, state)

Who? (informant)

What? (description)

When? (date)

8. George W. "Edson," untitled circular, 26 April 1898; George W. Edison invalid pension application no. 152,502, certificate no. 947,893; service of George W. Edison (Pvt., Co. D, 148th Ill. Inf., Civil War); Case Files of Approved Pension Applications . . . , 1861–1934; Civil War and Later Pension Files; Department of Veterans Affairs, Record Group (RG) 15; National Archives, Washington, D.C.

Where is? (repository, city, state)

Where in? (location details)

Physical sources viewed as images

We often use digital images, microfilm, or other media to view facsimiles of physical sources. Four combinations of published and unpublished physical sources and published and unpublished media are possible:

- *Published source viewed in a published medium*

  For example, a newspaper viewed online, on published microfilm, or on a CD-ROM; or images from a book or a National Archives microfilm publication viewed online

- *Published source viewed in an unpublished medium*

  For example, a published family history viewed on research or preservation microfilm, which includes most Family History Library microfilm

- *Unpublished source viewed in a published medium*

  For example, a birth register, deed book, gravestone, or probate file viewed online

- *Unpublished source viewed in an unpublished medium*

  For example, a probate file or marriage register viewed on Family History Library microfilm

Communicating information about both a physical source and the medium through which it was viewed is important in citations because information about the physical source communicates its evidence qualities, and information about the medium facilitates re-examination. Two-part citations (also called "layered" citations) reference both. Each part, separated by a semicolon, includes applicable Who-What-When-Where-Where elements of the published or unpublished source and those of the published or unpublished medium.

For examples and analysis of two-part citations, one each for the above four situations, see figures 3 and 4. For in-context examples of two-part citations to unpublished sources viewed in an unpublished medium, see the article in appendix A, footnotes 2, 6, and 25.

Sequencing citation elements

The great variability of genealogical sources complicates their citation formats and sequences, but one of two common patterns will work for many long-form reference-note citations. Elements and details then can be "subtracted" from the long-form citation to create logically sequenced short-form and source-list citations to the same source.

Most long-form citations to published sources follow a common sequence:

1. The *Who?* field—the publication's author—starts the citation.

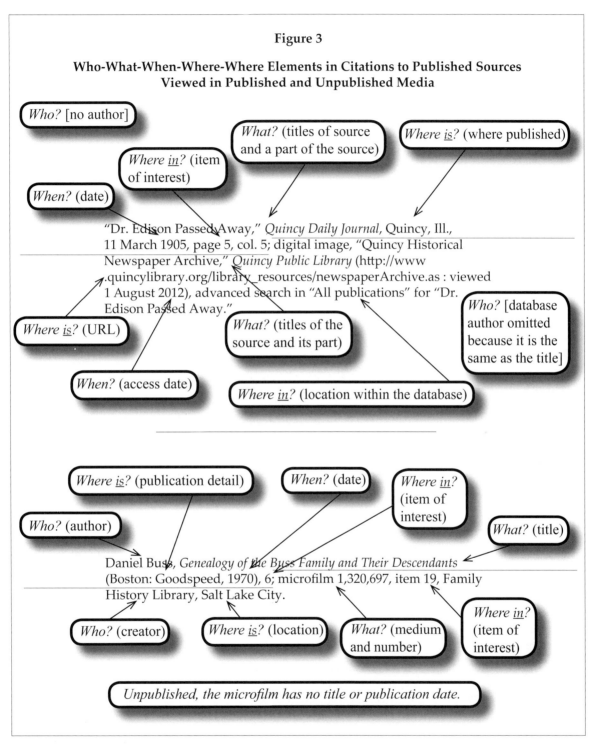

Figure 3

**Who-What-When-Where-Where Elements in Citations to Published Sources
Viewed in Published and Unpublished Media**

Who? [no author]

Where in? (item of interest)

What? (titles of source and a part of the source)

Where is? (where published)

When? (date)

"Dr. Edison Passed Away," *Quincy Daily Journal*, Quincy, Ill., 11 March 1905, page 5, col. 5; digital image, "Quincy Historical Newspaper Archive," *Quincy Public Library* (http://www .quincylibrary.org/library_resources/newspaperArchive.as : viewed 1 August 2012), advanced search in "All publications" for "Dr. Edison Passed Away."

Where is? (URL)

What? (titles of the source and its part)

Who? [database author omitted because it is the same as the title]

When? (access date)

Where in? (location within the database)

Where is? (publication detail)

When? (date)

Where in? (item of interest)

Who? (author)

What? (title)

Daniel Buss, *Genealogy of the Buss Family and Their Descendants* (Boston: Goodspeed, 1970), 6; microfilm 1,320,697, item 19, Family History Library, Salt Lake City.

Who? (creator)

Where is? (location)

What? (medium and number)

Where in? (item of interest)

Unpublished, the microfilm has no title or publication date.

Note: A semicolon separates each citation's two parts. Horizontal lines—for these instructional examples but not in actual practice—also separate the two parts and their respective element labels. The first citation is adapted from Thomas W. Jones, "Misleading Records Debunked: The Surprising Case of George Wellington Edison Jr.," *National Genealogical Society Quarterly* 100 (June 2012): 133–56.

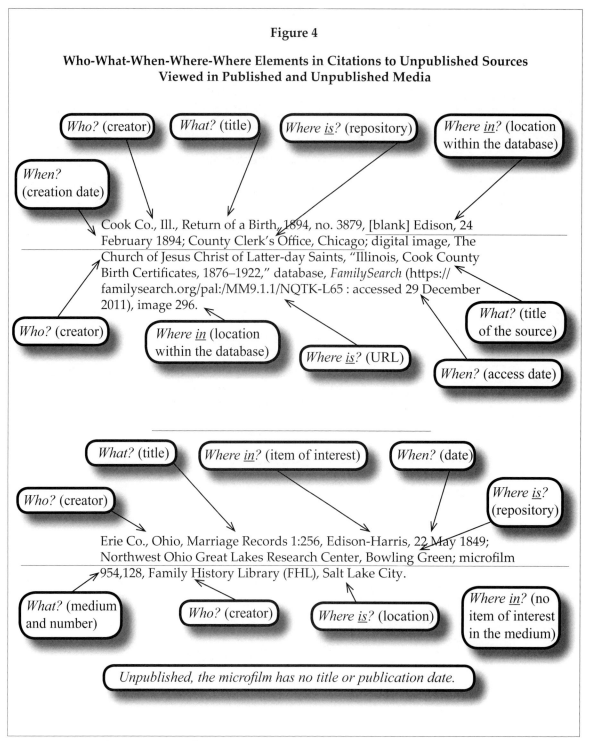

Figure 4

Who-What-When-Where-Where Elements in Citations to Unpublished Sources Viewed in Published and Unpublished Media

Who? (creator)   *What?* (title)   *Where is?* (repository)   *Where in?* (location within the database)

When? (creation date)

Cook Co., Ill., Return of a Birth, 1894, no. 3879, [blank] Edison, 24 February 1894; County Clerk's Office, Chicago; digital image, The Church of Jesus Christ of Latter-day Saints, "Illinois, Cook County Birth Certificates, 1876–1922," database, *FamilySearch* (https:// familysearch.org/pal:/MM9.1.1/NQTK-L65 : accessed 29 December 2011), image 296.

Who? (creator)   *Where in* (location within the database)   *Where is?* (URL)   *What?* (title of the source)   *When?* (access date)

What? (title)   *Where in?* (item of interest)   *When?* (date)

Who? (creator)   *Where is?* (repository)

Erie Co., Ohio, Marriage Records 1:256, Edison-Harris, 22 May 1849; Northwest Ohio Great Lakes Research Center, Bowling Green; microfilm 954,128, Family History Library (FHL), Salt Lake City.

What? (medium and number)   *Who?* (creator)   *Where is?* (location)   *Where in?* (no item of interest in the medium)

Unpublished, the microfilm has no title or publication date.

Note: A semicolon separates each citation's two parts. Horizontal lines—for these instructional examples but not in actual practice—also separate the two parts and their respective element labels. Citations are adapted from Jones, "Misleading Records Debunked," *National Genealogical Society Quarterly* 100 (June 2012): 133–56.

2. Next is the *What?* field, the source's italicized title, preceded by its part in quotation marks (only if a part needs to be cited) and followed by any needed descriptive information.

3. Next are the *Where is?* and *When?* fields in parentheses (except citations to newspapers usually omit parentheses).

4. The citation ends with the *Where in?* field—the page number or other item-locating detail.

The sequence of elements of citations to unpublished material also often is straightforward:

1. If the source's author, creator, or informant is known, the *Who?* field starts the citation. Parenthetical information about the author or creator's location might follow the name.

2. Next is the *What?* field—the name of the unpublished source, its description, or both.

3. The *When?* field may come next, if it is the unpublished source's or item's creation date.

4. Next is the *Where in?* field—identification of the item of interest and its location within the unpublished source.

5. The *When?* field may follow, if it is the date the event of interest occurred. If the preceding field includes levels, the date will follow the item it refers to.

6. Last is the *Where is?* field, including any sequence of layers—like collection, series, or record group—and ending with the repository and its city and state (or country, if outside the United States)

For examples of these sequences, see the citations in figures 1–4.

Kinds of citations

Genealogists writing proof statements, summaries, or arguments use citations primarily in two contexts:

- *Reference notes.* Documenting specific statements in narrative text or attached to images of source material, reference notes contain one or more citations. Most genealogical and word-processing programs number reference notes sequentially, using no number more than once. Each reference note's number corresponds to a superscripted number following the text segment that the note's citations document. Our software sequences reference notes according to our narrative's flow. Genealogical reference notes typically are footnotes, appearing at the bottoms of pages in a work-in-progress or finished genealogical product. In some contexts, however, instead of footnotes we may use endnotes, which appear at the end of an article or book. Whether presented as footnotes or endnotes, reference notes are a critical component of genealogical proof. For examples of reference notes in context, see the text and notes in the articles in appendixes A and B.

- *Source lists.* Similar to bibliographies and reference lists, source lists show research scope or the basis for an essay's content and direct others to sources of interest. Because source lists do not document specific statements, source-list citations do not contain all the specifics of a reference-note citation. Because source-list citations are not tied entry-by-entry to a narrative, we list them alphabetically by the citation's first word. Alternatively, we can group them by category, jurisdiction, or some other variable, and thereunder alphabetically. We number source lists typically only in contexts like lecture handouts, enabling speakers to refer to list items by number. For examples of source lists, see table 2 and this book's "Reading and Source List."

Within the broad reference-note and source-list contexts, genealogists use three kinds of citations—numbered below—each with its own format.

Reference notes

Citations in footnotes and endnotes use sentence style capitalization and punctuation. Each citation begins with a capital letter and ends with a period. Any internal periods appear only at the ends of abbreviations and within URLs. Within the citation we capitalize only proper nouns—names, places, and formal titles.

We often cite a source more than once in a finished product. The first citation uses a long-form format containing all citation elements. Subsequent citations to that source (even when specifics vary) will use an abbreviated, short-form reference-note citation format. (Following *Chicago* style, genealogists do not use *op. cit.* or other cross references between citations. We do, however, use *ibid.*—meaning *same as above*—to refer to the preceding citation).

Both long-form and short-form reference-note citations document specific statements within a narrative:

1. *Long-form citations.* Also called "full" reference-note citations, long-form citations contain all the who-what-when-where-where elements and media information described above. In finished products we use long-form citations only the first time we cite the source.

2. *Short-form citations.* Also called "subsequent" reference-note citations, short-form citations—usually less than a line long—serve to trigger the reader's recall of a prior corresponding long-form citation. We can create a short-form citation from a corresponding long-form citation by (1) listing only the author's surname and a shortened title—often its first few words, perhaps omitting a leading article (*A, An,* or *The*)— and (2) discarding information about publication, repository, and the medium in which we viewed the source. Item-of-interest detail will vary between long-form and corresponding short-form citations and within short-form citations to the same source, because we may repeatedly cite one source to document different statements about different people or events. Otherwise, short-form citations contain no

information not appearing in the corresponding long-form citation. We might not use short-form citations in works in progress, where the narrative's flow—and therefore the corresponding citations' sequence—is unstable.

See table 3 for examples of paired long-form and short-form citations. For mixed long-form and short-form citations in one reference note, see the article in appendix B, notes 33, 57, 64, and others.

Source lists

Unlike reference-note citations, source-list citations do not document specific statements. They also use a different format:

> 3. *Citations for source lists* are written paragraph style, customarily with a hanging indent. Each citation element is capitalized and punctuated sentence style, beginning with a capital letter and ending with a period—as if it were a sentence within a paragraph. We can create a source-list citation from a corresponding long-form reference-note citation by (*1*) changing the first author's name to a last-name-first format, (*2*) separating the citation elements with periods, (*3*) discarding parentheses (except those in journal and magazine citations), and (*4*) omitting item-of-interest details. For examples of source-list citations, see this chapter's table 2 and the book's "Reading and Source List."

Table 3

Long-Form and Short-Form Reference-Note Citations to the Same Source

LONG-FORM CITATION	SHORT-FORM CITATION
1. William Adams Simonds, *Edison: His Life, His Work, His Genius* (New York: Bobbs-Merrill, 1937), 337.	11. Simonds, *Edison*, 410.
2. "Brevities," *Quincy Daily Whig*, Quincy, Ill., 5 October 1882, page 8, col. 4.	12. "Brevities," 5 October 1882, page 8, col. 4.
3. "Katruska Family Tree," *Ancestry.com* (http://www.ancestry.com/ : viewed 1 August 2012).	13. "Katruska Family Tree."
4. Anne Bruner Eales and Robert M. Kvasnicka, *Guide to Genealogical Research in the National Archives of the United States* (Washington, D.C.: NARA, 2000), 26.	14. Eales and Kvasnicka, *Guide to Genealogical Research*, 197.
5. Jeanne Larzalere Bloom, CG, untitled report to Thomas W. Jones, 16 October 2011; files of Thomas W. Jones, Fairfax, Va.	15. Bloom, report to Jones.
6. J. J. Moran and Sons [undertakers], untitled mortuary record card, case no. 7927, 9 January 1940, George W. Edison; Moran and Goebel Funeral Home, Decatur, Ill.	16. Moran and Sons, untitled mortuary record card, no. 7927, George W. Edison.
7. "Family Record," printed form containing handwritten entries on both sides, likely 1920 or later and from a family Bible; photocopy from Howard Elting, Clinton, Utah; files of Thomas W. Jones, Fairfax, Va.	17. "Family Record," photocopy from Elting.

When and how to craft a citation

The best time to craft a citation is when looking at the source, but we may work on a citation at several points during our research planning, data collection, and afterward. Before examining the source we may use online catalogs and finding aids to create a full or partial citation for our research plan. When first examining the source—before becoming ensnared in searching for relevant information and evidence—we add to or refine that prior citation. As we work with the source we may incorporate further details to the citation, information about an item of interest, for example, or details the source bears that differ from its cataloguing. We may add comments about the source's contents and contexts and their implications for our research, conclusions, and proof. When writing our research results away from the source we may need to again consult online catalogs or finding aids to verify a questionable detail or obtain information we accidentally omitted from the citation while we had access to the source.

We also may need to gather citation details from several places. Even a book citation—perhaps the most straightforward and consistent of all citation formats—requires us to gather information from a book's title page, its copyright page, and the page or pages containing information relevant to our research. More complex sources may require information from library or publication catalogs or archival finding aids as well as information from different parts of the source and its physical or media context.

Resources for citing genealogical sources

Three publications give guidelines for citing genealogical work clearly and reliably:

1. *The BCG Genealogical Standards Manual* consolidates widely accepted genealogical research and compilation standards that evolved throughout the twentieth century. The standards include information about what to document and the style in which documentation should appear.[1]

2. The genealogical field has adopted the notes-and-bibliography-style reference-note format of *The Chicago Manual of Style*, now in its sixteenth edition, as the basis for genealogical documentation.[2] (The field does not follow other disciplines' style guides, like those of the American Psychological Association, Associated Press, and Modern Language Association.)[3]

---

1. Board for Certification of Genealogists, *The BCG Genealogical Standards Manual* (Orem, Utah: Ancestry, 2000). See especially page 3, standard 8 (the need for documentation); page 14, standard 36 (use of *Chicago* style); and page 18, standard 53 (what to document).

2. *The Chicago Manual of Style*, 16th ed. (Chicago: University of Chicago Press, 2010).

3. Board for Certification of Genealogists, *BCG Genealogical Standards Manual*, 14.

3. *Evidence Explained* expands *Chicago* style, which emphasizes citing published sources, for citations to myriad genealogical source material, including unpublished documents and artifacts. The book's first two chapters—required reading for serious genealogists—explain documentation and citation principles applicable to any genealogical source. The remaining chapters provide and explain model citations for hundreds of genealogical sources.[4] Genealogists who regularly cite sources find *Evidence Explained* indispensable. (*Evidence Explained* largely supersedes *Evidence!*, by the same author.)[5]

---

4. Elizabeth Shown Mills, *Evidence Explained: Citing History Sources from Artifacts to Cyberspace*, 2nd ed. (Baltimore: Genealogical Publishing, 2009). A PDF of this volume is available. See Elizabeth Shown Mills, *Evidence Explained: Historical Analysis, Citation, and Source Usage* (https://www.evidenceexplained.com/ : accessed 1 August 2012), "Book Store."

5. Elizabeth Shown Mills, *Evidence! Citation and Analysis for the Family Historian* (Baltimore: Genealogical Publishing, 1997).

Chapter 4 exercises

1. Why should genealogists cite sources completely and accurately?

2. Following the model, place in the table the elements of five additional reference-note citations to published sources from the articles in appendixes A and B:

    a.   Appendix A, note 7, the last citation

    b.   Appendix A, note 8, the last citation

    c.   Appendix A, note 36, the last citation

    d.   Appendix B, note 24, the last citation

    e.   Appendix B, note 28

    f.   Appendix B, note 70, the last citation

WHO?	WHAT?	WHEN?	WHERE IS?	WHERE IN?
a. Willis M. Kemper	*Genealogy of the Kemper Family . . .*	1899	Chicago: Geo. K. Hazlitt	page 79
b.				
c.				
d.				
e.				
f.				

3. Convert the same six long-form reference-note citations to short-form reference-note citations.

4. Convert the same six long-form reference-note citations to source-list citations.

5. Following the model, place in the table the elements of five additional reference-note citations to unpublished sources:

  a. Appendix A, note 4, first citation

  b. Appendix A, note 6

  c. Appendix A, note 16

  d. Appendix A, note 25 (ignoring the microfilm)

  e. Appendix B, note 6 (ignoring the microfilm)

  f. Appendix B, notes 11–12 (ignoring the microfilm)

WHO?	WHAT?	WHEN?	WHERE IN?	WHERE IS?
a. Kentucky Tax Assessor	Tax Books, Clark Co.	1793–1797, 1799–1809	1795, 6:25; and 1796, 2:21	Kentucky Historical Society, Frankfort
b.				
c.				
d.				
e.				
f.				

6. Convert the same six long-form reference-note citations to short-form reference-note citations.

7. Convert the same six long-form reference-note citations to source-list citations.

8. Suppose you quote a sentence on page 35 of this chapter. Write a long-form reference-note citation documenting the quotation's source.

9. Write a long-form reference-note citation to any journal or magazine article. If you read the article online, select an article with page numbers and write the citation as if you used the physical journal or magazine.

10. Search *Find A Grave* for George Tucker in Antrim County, Michigan. Click through to the page containing the "Memorial." Cite it with a long-form reference-note citation.

11. Write a long-form reference-note citation for the Web page at http://www.bcgcertification.org/resources/standard.html.

12. Following the model, separate each of the following double reference-note citations into its two parts and fill in the following table with each part's citation elements.

   a. Board for Certification of Genealogists, *The BCG Genealogical Standards Manual* (Orem: Utah: Ancestry, 2000), 1–2; digital images (incomplete), *Google Books* (http://books.google.com/books ?id=I0EgVqgKp6oC&printsec=frontcover&source=gbs_ge_summary_r&cad=0#v=onepage&q&f =false : viewed 1 August 2012).

   b. Van Buren Co., Mich., Return of Births in the County of Van Buren for the Year Ending December 31st, A.D. 1876, p. 256, no. 890, Carl McLain, 4 February; Department of Vital Records, Lansing; digital image, "Michigan Births, 1867–1902," *FamilySearch* (https://familysearch.org/pal:/ MM9.3.1/TH-267-12877-145173-47?cc=1459684 : viewed 1 August 2012).

   c. "List of all Passengers in Vessels from Foreign Ports Which Have Arrived at the Port of New Orleans during the Third Quarter of the Year 1832—and the Number That Have Died on the Passage," in *Quarterly Abstracts of Passenger Lists of Vessels Arriving at New Orleans, 1820–1875*, microfilm publication M272, 17 rolls (Washington, D.C.: National Archives and Records Service, 1969), roll 1, chronologically arranged, for "Brig Wm Osborne," 3 July 1832, Merdet entries; digital image, "New Orleans, Passenger List Quarterly Abstracts, 1820–1875," *Ancestry.com* (http://www.ancestry.com : downloaded 1 August 2012), search for "G Merdet."

WHO?	WHAT?	WHEN?	WHERE IS?	WHERE IN?
a1. Board for Certification of Genealogists	*The BCG Genealogical Standards Manual*	2000	Orem, Utah: Ancestry	pages 1–2
a2. [not applicable; creator has same name as title]	*Google Books*	1 August 2012	http://books.google.com/books?id=I0E gVqgKp6oC&printsec=frontcover&so urce=gbs_ge_summary_r&cad=0#v=o nepage&q&f=false	
b1.				
b2.				
c1.				
c2.				

13. If you do not have an account at *FamilySearch,* create one at https://ident
    .familysearch.org/cis-web/pages/registration/registration.html and sign
    in. Then write a double long-form reference-note citation documenting
    the physical source and digital image at https://familysearch.org/pal:/
    MM9.3.1/TH-566-11216-4918-97?cc=1320969.

14. Sign in at *FamilySearch,* and then write a double long-form reference-
    note citation documenting the physical source and digital image at
    https://familysearch.org/pal:/MM9.3.1/TH-1951-21742-22837-88?cc=
    1447693&wc=12205332.

15. Point your Web browser to http://archive.quincylibrary.org/Default/
    Skins/QPL/Client.asp?skin=QPL&AppName=2&AW=1343593579035,
    click "Advanced Archive Search," search the *Quincy Daily Herald*
    for "Edison," and write a double long-form reference-note citation
    documenting the physical source and digital image that you see.

Check your answers at the back of the book.

Chapter 5

GPS Element 3: Analysis and Correlation

Only tests of analysis and correlation help us reliably prove which sources and information and evidence items are likely right and which are not.

No genealogical source bears a credible guarantee of accuracy. Any source's information can be entirely right or entirely wrong, or the source may contain a mixture of correct and incorrect information—a common scenario. When we use a single source's information as evidence—as nothing more than a tentative answer—that answer also may be right or wrong. Proof, of course, requires us to determine which sources, information items, and evidence items are probably correct and which are not. Consequently, we must test our sources, information, and evidence.

Some tests are invalid or insufficient. Categorical judgments, for example, are risky. Errors exist in every category of source: censuses, genealogies (both online and in print), deeds, military rosters, religious records, tax rolls, wills, and other kinds of genealogical materials. For examples, see table 4. Similarly, categorical judgments based on a compiler's reputation also include risk. Authors of genealogies and compilers of records are human—thus imperfect—and their work may contain errors.

Only testing helps us reliably determine which sources and information and evidence items are likely right or wrong. Genealogists use the processes of analysis and correlation to test the accuracy of evidence and potential conclusions. One process is insufficient. We must both analyze and correlate.

Tests of analysis

We analyze one source at a time. Two analytical tests are fundamental: (*1*) determining whether the source is an authored work or an original or derivative record; and (*2*) determining—if we can—whether each relevant information item is primary or secondary. Analysis also includes asking— and answering—questions about the source's physical characteristics, its content, its informant or informants, its purpose, its history, and its

Table 4

Selected Documented Examples of Errors in High-Quality Sources

ERRONEOUS SOURCE	DOCUMENTATION
Baptismal register with a wrong birth date	Melinda Daffin Henningfield, "Determining Linnie Leigh Gray's Birth Date," *National Genealogical Society Quarterly* 98 (December 2010): 245–50.
Birth record with an incorrect surname	Teri D. Tillman, "Using Indirect Evidence and Linguistic Analysis to Trace Polin Ries of New Orleans," *National Genealogical Society Quarterly* 99 (December 2011): 245–74.
Death record with parent's name incorrect	Allen R. Peterson, "Who were the Parents of Charlotte Ann Williams of Flint, Michigan? A Death Certificate with a Half-Truth," *National Genealogical Society Quarterly* 98 (September 2010): 177–88.
Family Bible record with fabricated information	Warren L. Forsythe, "Resolving Conflict between Records: A Spurious Moseley Bible," *National Genealogical Society Quarterly* 84 (September 1996): 182–99.
Marriage bond falsely identifying a bride's late husband	Richard A. Hayden, "Resolving the Inexplicable: The Marriage Bond of Archibald Young and Lettice Morgan," *National Genealogical Society Quarterly* (March 2007): 5–16.
Four marriage license applications misidentifying bride's or groom's father	Thomas W. Jones, "'A Solid Gang of Them': An Illinois Morse-Trammell Family's Reactions to Scandal," *National Genealogical Society Quarterly* 92 (June 2004): 105–18.
Military records omitting a soldier	Harold E. Hinds Jr., "The Man Who Wasn't There: Harold Bion Wiltse (1896–1972) and the World War I 'Lost Battalion,'" *National Genealogical Society Quarterly* 97 (June 2010): 101–10.
Quitclaim worded as a fee-simple deed with an incomplete land description	Thomas W. Jones, "Uncovering Ancestors by Deduction: The Husbands and Parents of Eleanor (née Medley) (Tureman) (Crow) Overton," *National Genealogical Society Quarterly* 94 (December 2006): 287–305.
Tax rolls listing a dead man as a living taxpayer	Ibid.
Will omitting testator's eleven children and falsely identifying three heirs	Thomas W. Jones, "The Children of Calvin Snell: Primary versus Secondary Evidence," *National Genealogical Society Quarterly* 83 (March 1995): 17–31.

Note: Table from Thomas W. Jones, "Source Snobbery," *OnBoard: Newsletter of the Board for Certification of Genealogists* (May 2012): 9–10 and 15.

provenance. Analysis does not show whether a specific information item is right or wrong, but it does reveal whether a source is more or less likely to contain errors.

Authored work or original or derivative record?

When a record is based on altering or processing a prior source—creating an abstract, transcription, or translation, for example—it is derived from that record. The human or machine creating the derivative probably misread, miswrote, misinterpreted, or omitted some of the record's information, making the derivative record less accurate than the original.

Authored works are more than derivative sources, which process information from one or a few sources. Authors typically draw from many diverse sources, and they use them to develop conclusions, interpretations, and ideas that exist nowhere except in their own authored work. Although authored works may comprise large amounts of material that exists nowhere else, authors may have misinterpreted some of their sources, or flawed reasoning may have led to an erroneous conclusion, interpretation, or idea.

Source categories usually are unambiguous. Authored works typically synthesize information from diverse sources to create new knowledge. Derivative records usually are designed to increase accessibility to information in original records. With some exceptions, a record's derivation from a prior record is clear. Genealogists often easily—sometimes automatically—make these distinctions.

When we examine a source and its context, we determine whether it is an authored work or an original or derivative record. We note the source's physical characteristics. Consistent handwriting, ink, writing utensil, and paper may indicate a copy—a derivative. Certification as a copy indicates a derivative. A printing or copyright date long after the record date, a certification date long after the recorded event date, or physical characteristics inconsistent with record dates, may indicate a derivative. Abstracts, translations, and handwritten and typed transcriptions, both online and in print, are obvious derivative records.

Source analysis will include facsimiles of physical sources—for example, digital photos, microfilm, online images, photocopies, and scans. If the facsimile bears no sign of alteration we assess it as we would assess the underlying physical source, which could be either an authored work or an original or derivative record. Only if an image bears evidence of alteration—cropping or blurring, for example—would we assess the image as a derivative and need to pursue the original.

We also note the source's history and provenance—information that may appear within the source, perhaps in its introduction or other front matter, or in its repository's catalog or finding aid. Descriptive details may reveal whether the source is authored, an original record, or a record derived from an original.

We prefer original records (and facsimiles of original records) because they are less vulnerable to error than derivative records and authored works. Genealogical proof requires support from the least error-prone sources that are relevant and available. When we determine that a source is derived from another source we attempt to locate that source. If it no longer exists, we can use the derivative to support our genealogical proof, but we do so with more caution than when we can base proof entirely on original sources.

Primary, secondary, or indeterminable information?

Informants who report events they did not witness create secondary information. Eyewitness reports of events are primary information. Because retelling often introduces error into an account, secondary information is more error-prone than primary information.

Determining whether an information item is primary or secondary requires us to understand (1) who the item's informant was, and (2) how the informant acquired that information. We also must distinguish informants from recorders—officials writing information that someone tells them are not informants. Sometimes these determinations are easy to make, sometimes they are difficult, and sometimes they are impossible.

Many sources identify informants directly and give us enough detail to determine whether their information is primary or secondary.

- Signatures sometimes identify informants indirectly.

- Religious officiants signing records likely provide primary information about a marriage or burial date and place, but their information about the parties' parentage and ages may be secondary.

- Authors of wills provide primary information about their property and heirs.

- Sellers of land signing a deed give primary information about their ownership and neighbors and the property's drainage, but the deed's technical land description from an unnamed surveyor likely is secondary information.

- Witnesses, providing primary information, certify they saw a testator or grantor sign a will or deed.

- Signers of accounts, affidavits, applications, bonds, inventories, and various kinds of returns typically provide primary information.

- Physicians, sextons, and recorders provide primary information items for death certificates. A designated informant, however, likely provided secondary information about a deceased person's birth and parentage and perhaps primary information about the deceased person's occupation.

Sometimes we can deduce an unnamed informant's identity from the information and its context:

- A new parent likely provided the *parent* information for a birth or baptismal certificate, even though only a physician, midwife, or religious official signed it.

- Even if a marriage bond bears only an official's signature, the prospective groom likely specified his intent to marry.

- A farmer or merchant likely kept his own accounts, though he might not have signed them.

- Specific dates or ages may point to an unnamed but identifiable informant, if only one person is likely to know those details.

Sometimes, as with pre-1940 American censuses, the informant is unknown. This prevents us from classifying the information as primary or secondary, making it indeterminable.

The primary/secondary/indeterminable-information distinction offers complexities that the authored/original/derivative-source distinction does not. Authored, original, and derivative refer to an entire source, but one source may have several informants, and each informant may provide primary, secondary, or indeterminable information items or some of each. Also, determining whether a source is authored, original, or derivative is easier than determining whether an information item is primary or secondary. Consequently, while we usually can discern whether a source is authored, original, or derivative, we may be unable to determine whether some information items are primary or secondary.

We prefer primary information because it is less vulnerable to error than secondary information, and support for genealogical proof should include direct, indirect, or negative evidence from at least one eyewitness. When we determine that an information item is secondary we attempt to locate an eyewitness's information. If it does not exist, we can use secondary information, but we do so with more caution than when we can base proof solely on primary information.

Other tests of analysis

Besides determining whether a source is authored, original, or derivative and whether relevant information items are primary or secondary, analysis also includes asking—and answering—questions about the source's physical characteristics, its content, its informant or informants, its purpose, its history, and its provenance. Answers to these questions may help us detect intentional and accidental errors and to form an opinion about a source's likely accuracy:

- Why was the source was created?

    Sources created for routine business, governmental, or religious purposes are more likely correct than sources created for purposes of personal prestige, social status, financial gain, or other benefit.

- What was the time lapse between the events a source reports and its creation?

    As time passes memory fades and errors become more likely. Records created soon after events are more likely accurate.

- Was the author or record keeper professional and careful?

    Professional or trained record keepers—like census takers, clerks, and public and religious officials—are more likely to record information correctly than a private individual unaccustomed to record keeping. Obvious errors, omissions, or corrections also will raise questions about an author's or recorder's ability to create an accurate record.

- Was the source open to challenge and correction?

    Information subjected to challenge or cross examination, like documents presented in court, are more likely accurate than information prepared and used privately. If an informant reviewed a written statement, perhaps swearing an oath of accuracy, the information is more likely accurate than a record the informant did not review.

- Were the source and information protected against bias, fraud, and tampering?

    Sources subjected to legal protections (like examination by a judge and cross examination by lawyers) and physical protections (like access restrictions and secure storage) are more likely accurate than sources not subjected to these protections.

- If the source is authored, did experts evaluate it?

    Publications subjected to vetting likely are more accurate than published material that no expert evaluated.

- If the source is authored, did the writer use the least error-prone sources or works and authors with less reliability?

- Does the source show a sign of alteration at any point in its history?

    Alteration, while possibly the correction of an error, also suggests the possibility of deception or fraud. In any case, alterations made significantly later than a source's creation may be vulnerable to memory errors or misinterpretations.

- Does the informant or author show potential for bias?

    Information provided for personal gain or enhanced status is suspect.

- Was the informant reliable as both observer and reporter?

  Reports of events viewed through children's eyes may be less accurate than reports by adult witnesses. Reports by people with poor memory may be less accurate than those reported by people with good memory.

Tests of correlation

Genealogical correlation is a process of comparing and contrasting. When we correlate we show or discuss items in agreement and items in disagreement. Evidence items in agreement may become conclusions. Disagreeing evidence items conflict. If we cannot resolve the conflicts (see chapter 6), we will not have a conclusion.

Prerequisite to correlation

Sources and information may be either independent of each other or related. Independent items may be successfully correlated, but correlation of related items will yield an invalid result:

- Related sources and information can be traced back to one author, record, or informant.

  Suppose, for example, we discover the same birth date on a death certificate and a gravestone. If that date came from a family Bible record, the information items from the gravestone, certificate, and Bible are related, not independent. Related information items provide no corroboration; they merely duplicate one another. Consequently, when we correlate, we group related information items together, giving them the credibility of the most likely accurate of the grouped sources and informants providing the related information. Thus, we would group the gravestone, death certificate, and family Bible record's information together as if they were one source, and we would give it the credibility of the family Bible, the birth date's earliest recording.

- Independent sources and information items arise from separate prior sources or informants.

  For example, a census during childhood, a draft registration card in early adulthood, and a death certificate, each providing a man's age, likely are independent. An adult likely provided the age for the childhood census, the person of interest provided it for the draft card, and a surviving spouse, offspring, or sibling for the death record. If each informant based the age on his or her observation or experience, these sources and their age information would be independent of one other. When we compare them and find they agree on a birth year, the agreement suggests the year accurately reflects the time of birth.

Ways to correlate

Tests of correlation and their formats range from simple to complex:

- With a few sources and mostly direct evidence, we may almost automatically recognize points of agreement and disagreement.

  Suppose, for example, two marriage records identify the father of bride Mary L. Jones as Silas Jones, Mary L. appears in Silas's 1860 household, and Hullum Jones's will names his granddaughter, "Louisiana," daughter of his late son, Silas. We see evidence of the same father-daughter connection four times, even though the daughter's name in the will differs from that in the other sources.

- More complicated cases, with many sources and different kinds of evidence, require us to write about the evidence, comparing and contrasting evidence items in narrative sentences or bullet points. This writing or listing helps us see points of similarity and conflict.

  For an example, see table 5, which compares sources to show that a groom gave false information for his marriage record.

- Correlated points arranged chronologically form a timeline.

  For an example, see table 6.

- When we have a large number of evidence items we use tables or spreadsheets to reveal parallels and conflicts in information and evidence.

  See table 7. The vertical axis of such arrays often forms a timeline.

- Showing or platting locations on a map also may compare genealogical evidence about places or tracts of land.

  For an example, see figure 5.

When to analyze and correlate

We analyze sources and information one source at a time as we plan research, during our research's data collection phases, and after the research is complete. As we examine a source and its prefatory and cataloging information, we note whether the source is an authored work or an original or derivative record. Our working notes' citations to each source may reflect these distinctions, or we may annotate the citations. We also identify informants for information items of interest and try to understand whether or not they are eyewitnesses. Again, our working notes' citations may reflect the primary/secondary/indeterminable-information distinction, or we may annotate our notes. Similarly, our notes, citations, and annotations may reflect or incorporate answers to other analytical questions about our sources and their potentially relevant information items.

As our research progresses and we encounter authored works, derivative sources, and secondary or indeterminable information, we extend our

---

Table 5

Illustration of Correlation in a Narrative and a List

On 22 November 1887 Ida Hall married George Emberson Floyd in Litchfield, Illinois, about 150 miles southeast of Quincy. Certifying "the information above given is correct," Floyd said he was twenty-nine, native to Alexander County, Illinois, son of Joseph D. and Mary Manerva Floyd, and not previously married.[1] He lied. George Emberson Floyd was George W. Edison:

- Floyd's bride, Ida Hall, was born on 28 November 1871. Because Ida was too young to marry without parental permission, Telithi Holmesley—identifying herself and her ex-husband, Oliver Hall, as Ida's parents—consented to the marriage.[2] Ida said her birthplace was "Boon" County, Arkansas.[3]
- In 1932 Ida Tankersley's widowed husband, Marion, said Ida, daughter of "Olliver" Hall and "[blank] Homelsey" was born at Harrison, Arkansas, on 28 November 1872.[4] Harrison is a Boone County, Arkansas, township. Therefore, Ida Tankersley's maiden name, birthplace, age, and parents are those of George Emberson Floyd's bride.
- Marion Tankersley had married Ida Edison in Phelps County, Missouri, on 5 September 1915.[5] Edison stepchildren—Harris O., nineteen, and Beulah A., sixteen—lived in the Tankersley household in 1920.[6]
- In Phelps County on 10 May 1912—three years before marrying Marion Tankersley—Ida divorced George W. Edison. She received custody of their four living children: Howard, twenty; Thomas and Harris, eleven; and Beulah, eight.[7]
- The 1900 and 1910 censuses agree that Ida and George W. Edison had married in 1886–87.[8] If the censuses are correct, and if George Edison was not George Emberson Floyd, Ida Hall married Floyd on 22 November 1887 and Edison before 31 December 1887, an improbable scenario.
- George and Ida Edison's first child, Theresia, was born in July 1889, about twenty months after Ida had married George Emberson Floyd.[9] If Edison were not Floyd and Theresia's conception, about November 1888, followed her parents' marriage, Ida would have married twice within thirteen months, a remote possibility.
- Illinois's 1763–1900 marriage index references no George Edison–Ida Hall marriage.[10]
- Census indexes offer no candidates for George Emberson Floyd and his alleged parents, Joseph and Mary Floyd, in Alexander County, Illinois, or elsewhere in 1860, 1870, and 1880.[11]

---

1. Montgomery Co., Ill., marriage file 8386, for Marriage License: Minor, signed by George E. Floyd, Ida Floyd, and Justice of the Peace W. C. Henderson; County Clerk's Office, Hillsboro, Ill.

2. Ibid., for Telithi A. Holmesley to John J. McLean (Circuit Clerk), letter, 19 November 1887. Telithi signed the letter, written by someone else on the letterhead of "C. A. Oller, Attorney and Counselor at Law," Litchfield, Ill. In 1880 Ida lived with her parents near Litchfield but across a county line. See 1880 U.S. census, Macoupin Co., Ill., pop. sch., ED 112, Carlinville, p 26, dwell. 252, fam. 257, Oliver Hall household; NARA microfilm T9, roll 232.

3. Montgomery Co., Ill., marriage file 8386, for Marriage License: Minor.

4. Missouri Division of Health, Standard Certificate of Death, no. 36678, Ida Tankersley; PDF, Missouri Secretary of State, *Missouri State Archives: Missouri Death Certificates, 1910–1960*, for Ida Tankersley, Phelps Co.

5. Phelps Co., Mo., Marriage License Record 9:158, Tankersley-Edison, filed 7 September 1915; Recorder of Deeds, Rolla, Mo.; FHL microfilm 914,755.

6. 1920 U.S. census, Phelps Co., Mo., pop. sch., Newburg City, Arlington Twp., ED 66, sheet 1B, dwell. 15, fam. 16, Marion "Tankersly" household; NARA microfilm T625, roll 941.

7. Phelps Co., Mo., Book V:353–54, Edison v. Edison; Genealogical Department, Old Courthouse, Rolla, Mo.

8. 1900 U.S. census, St. Louis Co., Mo., pop. sch., City of St. Louis, ED 412, sheet 7B, dwell. 123, fam. 140, George W. Edison household. Also, 1910 U.S census, Greene Co., Mo., pop. sch., Springfield City, ward 6, ED 37, sheet 10B, dwell. 208, fam. 229, George W. "Eddison" household; NARA microfilm T624, roll 782.

9. "Family Record," printed form containing handwritten entries on both sides, likely 1920 or later and from a family Bible; photocopy from Howard Elting, Clinton, Utah; author's files. Mr. Elting received the record from his aunt, daughter of Howard Edison, George and Ida's son. See Elting to author, e-mail, 24 October 2011.

10. See "Illinois Statewide Marriage Index, 1763–1900," database, *Illinois State Archives*, searches of Edison grooms and Hall brides.

11. "Census and Voter Lists," database, *Ancestry.com*, searches for Emberson and Floyd surnames in Illinois in 1860, 1870, and 1880 United States censuses.

Note: The above is excerpted from Thomas W. Jones, "Misleading Records Debunked: The Surprising Case of George Wellington Edison Jr.," *National Genealogical Society Quarterly* 100 (June 2012): 141–42.

Table 6

Timeline Separating the Identities of Men Named John Geddes in the Same Irish Parish

DATE	EVENT	SOURCE	IDENTITIES AND LIFE SPANS		
1735–39	Named as vestryman	Vestry minutes	John Geddes, born about 1700; died in 1746–66		
1740	Named as freeholder	List of Protestant freeholders			
1740–46	Named as vestryman	Vestry minutes			
1766	Named	Protestant census		John Geddes, born in 1736–37; died in 1798	
1775	Signed a Petition	Petition			
1781	Widow Geddes held a lease for the life of John Geddes, age 44 (born 1736–37)	Rent roll			
1796	1 wheel	Flax Seed Premiums			
1796	Two John Geddeses named	List of freeholders			John Geddes, born about 1770
1798	Testator and heir both named John Geddes	Will of John Geddes			
1800–13	Baptisms of five children	Baptismal records			
1826	Assessed for taxes	Tax list			

For details, see Thomas W. Jones, "Organizing Meager Evidence to Reveal Lineages: An Irish Example— Geddes of Tyrone," *National Genealogical Society Quarterly* 89 (June 2001): 98–112.

Figure 5

Map Correlating Evidence from Ten Deeds, a Chancery Case, and a Land Grant to Help Prove a Relationship

Bedford County, Virginia, Tracts Associated with Mitchell, Pratt, and Witt

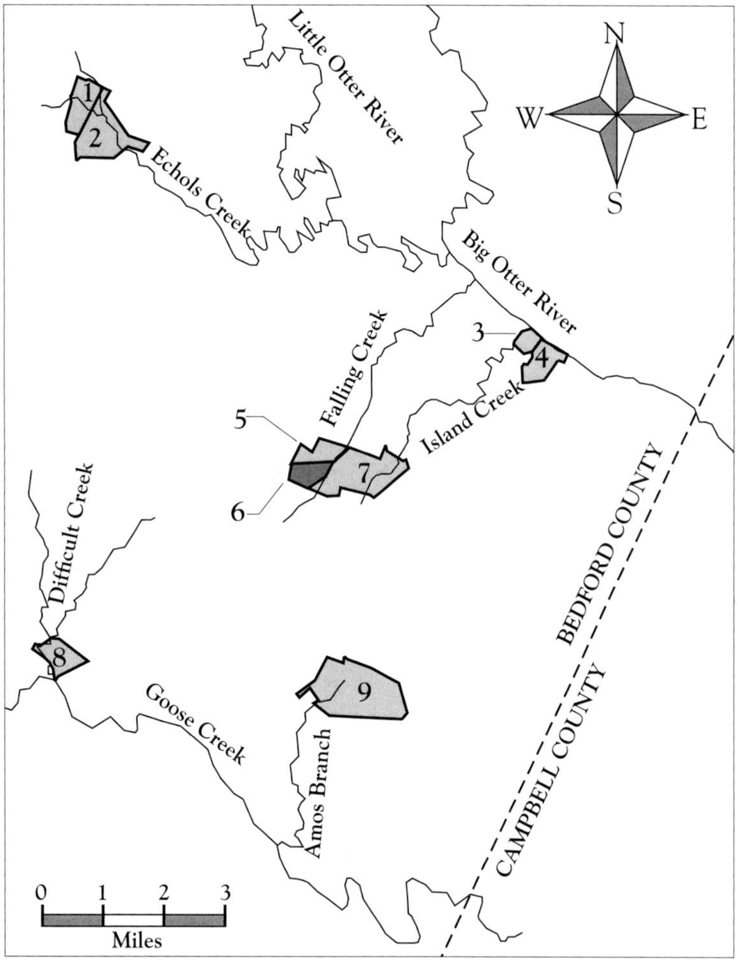

Notes: Map drawn by Warren C. Pratt. See original text for documentation of landowners' and neighbors' locations.

Key: Tract 1—Jesse Witt (father of Henry)
         Tract 2—Rowland Witt, later Mills Witt
         Tracts 3 and 4—Anne Witt (mother of Jesse)
         Tracts 5 and 6—Enos Mitchell (Elizabeth Pratt's master)
         Tract 7—Grant to Benjamin Witt
         Tract 8—Robert Witt
         Tract 9—James Pratt (Elizabeth Pratt's father's uncle), whose widow was Mary

Note: figure from Warren C. Pratt, "Finding the Father of Henry Pratt of Southeastern Kentucky," *National Genealogical Society Quarterly* 100 (June 2012): 85–103, figure 2 from p. 101. The author thanks Dr. Pratt for his permission to reprint this figure.

research to locate corresponding original records and primary information or to determine that it does not exist. The need to use the most accurate source available demands this pursuit of original records and primary information. When a corresponding original record or primary information item no longer exists, then we meet the standard with an authored or derivative source or secondary or indeterminable information item.

We may correlate information items as our research progresses, but correlation results are most useful when the correlation includes all available evidence items relevant to our research question. The best time to correlate is after we have finished identifying and examining relevant sources, gathering information items from them, and considering their possibilities as direct, indirect, and negative evidence.

Outcomes of analysis and correlation

Analysis shows whether a source's information is more or less likely to be correct. Correlation shows how that information and the resulting evidence resembles or differs from other information and evidence items. Together they may lead to proof.

Casting doubt

Assessing a record as derivative or an information item as secondary causes us to question the accuracy of its evidence. We similarly cast doubt on evidence—a tentative answer—when we cannot corroborate it. Casting doubt on evidence or information sometimes is described as "giving it lesser weight."

Suppose, for example, three sources show Zerviah Burton was born in Vermont and one source shows she was born in New York. Absent corroboration, the New York information's accuracy is doubtful. Doubt increases if the uncorroborated birthplace evidence comes from secondary information, a derivative record, or an authored work.

Resolve conflicts

Source and information qualities and correlation can resolve conflicting evidence. Lack of corroboration for one side of a conflict, for example, may indicate the information is incorrect. Similarly, we may resolve a conflict in favor of eyewitness information in an original record. For examples and further information, see chapter 6.

Yield conclusions

Evidence is a tentative answer to a genealogical question. When we test an answer with analysis and correlation, it becomes a hypothesis. If the hypothesis passes the tests, it becomes a conclusion.

The most important outcome of analysis and correlation is an established conclusion. Information in agreement, especially primary information from original records, is likely correct. Uncorroborated information, especially secondary information from derivative records, may be wrong. Such error may be especially likely when primary-information items from original records agree on a different answer.

For example, the correlation in table 5 (showing a narrative and a list) supports the conclusion that a bridegroom provided a false identity for his marriage record. The correlation in table 7, along with other data, helps support a conclusion that George Edison, Edwin Wellman, and Edwin Edison were the same man.

Table 7

A Table Correlating Sources, Information, and Evidence

George Wellington Edison Jr. in Federal Censuses				
YEAR AND PLACE	NAME	BIRTH YEAR AND PLACE	FATHER'S BIRTHPLACE	MOTHER'S BIRTHPLACE
1870 Quincy, Illinois	George W. Eddison	1860–61 Illinois	Canada	Ohio[a]
1880 Quincy, Illinois	George Edison	1860–61 Illinois	Canada	Ohio[b]
1900 St. Louis, Missouri	George W[.] Edison	Nov 1861 Missouri	Missouri	Missouri[c]
1910 Springfield, Missouri	George W. Eddison	1864–65 Illinois	Kansas	Kansas[d]
1920 Evansville, Indiana	Edwin Wellman	1859–60 Ohio	Ohio	Ohio[e]
1930 Decatur, Illinois	Edwin Edison	1860–61 Illinois	~~Scotch~~ English Canada	Ohio[f]

a. 1870 U.S. census, Adams Co., Ill., Quincy, ward 5, p. 27, dwelling 196, family 218; National Archives and Records Administration (NARA) microfilm publication M593, roll 187.

b. 1880 U.S. census, Adams Co., Ill., pop. sch., Quincy, enumeration district (ED) 31, p. 14, dwell./fam. 131; NARA microfilm T9, roll 175.

c. 1900 U.S. census, St. Louis Co., Mo., pop. sch., City of St. Louis, ED 412, sheet 7B, dwell. 123, fam. 140; NARA microfilm T623, roll 901.

d. 1910 U.S census, Greene Co., Mo., pop. sch., Springfield City, ward 6, ED 37, sheet 10B, dwell. 208, fam. 229; NARA microfilm T624, roll 782.

e. 1920 U.S. census, Vanderburgh Co., Ind., pop. sch., Evansville, ED 127, sheet 14A, dwell. 283, fam. 331; NARA microfilm T625, roll 471.

f. 1930 U.S. census, Macon Co., Ill., pop. sch., Decatur, ED 58-5, sheet 8B, dwell. 149, fam. 219; NARA microfilm T626, roll 537.

Note: Excerpted and adapted from Jones, "Misleading Records Debunked," *NGS Quarterly* 100 (June 2012): 150.

Chapter 5 exercises

1. Using the Bible record citation in appendix B, note 2, and the image from that source on the page opposite, answer the following questions:

    a. Is the source an authored work, original record, or derivative record?

    b. Is the record's informant known? If so, who is it?

    c. Is the information about Earl McLain's birth date primary information, secondary information, or indeterminable?

    d. Suppose your research question is *When was Earl McLain born?* Does this source provide direct, indirect, or negative evidence? What answer does that evidence provide?

    e. Suppose your research question is *When did Ida divorce Charles D. McLain?* Does this source provide direct, indirect, or negative evidence? What answer does that evidence provide?

    f. Why was this source created?

    g. Was there a time lapse between Earl's birth and this source's creation? Why do you think so?

    h. Was the record keeper careful?

    i. Was the source open to challenge, verification, or correction?

    j. Was the source protected against bias, fraud, and tampering?

    k. Was the informant reliable as both observer and reporter, or did he or she show potential for bias or other factors affecting reliability?

    l. What do your answers tell you about this source's usefulness and credibility as a provider of genealogical evidence?

Census images and citations for Question 2

Don Higele	38	m	bricklayer			do
Barb	do	24	f			do
Ad	do	5	m			do
Trif	do	4	m			do
Joh	do	2	m			do
Marie	do	½	f			do
Corn	do	23	m	bricklayer		Germ

Source: 1850 U.S. census, St. Louis Co., Mo., ward 1, fo. 94v, dwelling 1082, family 1676, "Don Higele" household, born in "Germ"; National Archives and Records Administration (NARA) microfilm publication M432, roll 415.

Antoine Higley	50	m	Stone Mason	800	100	Hanover
Barba	"	33	f			"
Adolph	"	14	m			"
Fred	"	13	"			"
Mary	"	11	f			"
Sipha	"	9	"			"
Jacob	"	6	m			Illinois
Tessie	"	3	f			"

Source 1860 U.S. census, Randolph Co., Ill., Township 4 South Range 8 W, Red Bud post office, p. 144, dwelling 1075, family 1076, "Antoine Higley" household; NARA microfilm M653, roll 221.

2. Use the form below to construct a table correlating evidence of names, ages, occupations, and birthplaces from the two census images shown on the facing page. Then comment on what the correlated evidence reveals about identities, relationships, and migration.

1850 CENSUS (MISSOURI)	1860 CENSUS (ILLINOIS)

Commentary:

3. Following the model, use the article in appendix A to identify an example of each correlation format discussed in this chapter (page 60) showing points of agreement or disagreement and to comment on conclusions that each correlation supports or negates.

TYPE	LOCATION IN ARTICLE AND CONTENT	COMMENTS ON CONCLUSIONS
Narrative	*The article's page 29, bottom of page; compares census and tax lists*	*Tax lists and censuses agree on Philip's approximate age.*
Narrative		
List		
Timeline		
Table		
Map		

4. Following the model, use the article in appendix B to identify an example of each correlation format discussed in this chapter showing points of agreement or disagreement and to comment on conclusions that each correlation supports or negates.

TYPE	LOCATION IN ARTICLE AND CONTENT	COMMENTS ON CONCLUSIONS
Narrative	*The first paragraph under "Another Woman's Husband" on the article's pages 105–6 compares direct and negative evidence from the 1900 census with direct evidence from Charles and Ida's marriage record.*	*The discussion shows points of both agreement and disagreement between the two sources. Evidence elsewhere in the article shows the two sources pertain to the same man.*
Narrative		
List		
Timeline		
Table		
Map		

Check your answers at the back of the book.

Chapter 6

GPS Element 4:
Resolving Conflicts and Assembling Evidence

If we cannot resolve the conflict, we have no conclusion to prove.

Conflicting evidence items provide incompatible answers to the same question. For example, some evidence indicates Eleanor's father was George Samuel Klug, and other evidence suggests he was Jacob Medley. At least one of those answers is wrong. Such conflicts can involve any of the data genealogists examine, including date, name, occupation, place, relationship, religion, and socioeconomic status. Some conflicts are major, some are minor, and some are between.

Ignoring a conflict calls our research, reasoning, and conclusion into question. Major conflicts must be resolved. We should avoid, however, over-emphasizing minor conflicts or obvious errors. Instead, we note them in passing—for example, a minor birth-date discrepancy that has no bearing on the research conclusion. For an instance of noting a conflict in passing, see appendix B (the article's page 106, the last two sentences of the second paragraph).

"Resolution of conflicting evidence" is the only GPS element we may bypass. If thorough research produces only evidence items agreeing on the answer to our research question, or compatible with that answer, we have no conflict to resolve. Thus, we sometimes can meet the GPS without addressing element 4.

We must, however, resolve evidence conflicting with a potential conclusion before we can finalize it and advance our case to proof. Unresolved conflicting evidence is incompatible with a conclusion. Until we resolve the conflict, we have no case for proof. A proved conclusion rests on all valid applicable evidence resulting from a thorough search, not part of it. Resolution requires us to establish that some part of the collected evidence is incorrect or does not apply to the research question at hand.

How evidence conflicts

Genealogical evidence items may conflict in any combination:

1. *A direct-evidence item may conflict with another direct-evidence item.*

   For example, when the research question is "Who did Emma Cope marry?," one online source specifies the answer "Charles D. McLain" and another says " David R. McLain." See appendix B, the article's page 107.

2. *A direct-evidence item may conflict with an indirect-evidence item or a negative-evidence item (or vice versa).*

   For example, when the research question is "Who was Amzi Leach's father?," direct evidence says his father was Benjamin or John Leach and indirect evidence from other sources suggests he was Abraham Leach or Daniel Wallen. For details, see Thomas W. Jones, "The Four Fathers of Amzi Leach: Analysis of Conflicting Evidence," *National Genealogical Society Quarterly* 82 (September 1994): 207–15 .

3. *An indirect-evidence or negative-evidence item may conflict with another indirect-evidence item or a negative-evidence item.*

   For example, when the question is *Where did plaintiff Philip Pritchett live?*, his initiating a lawsuit in Fauquier County implies he lived there, but no Pritchett appears in the county tax lists around that time, implying he lived elsewhere. See the article in appendix A, pages 30–33.

Resolving conflicting evidence

When evidence conflicts, we have incompatible answers to a research question. Resolving the conflict requires us to separate the evidence into likely-correct and likely-incorrect answers, discard the incorrect answers, and justify or explain that separation and discarding.

Reasoning

We may resolve conflicting answers to research questions in one, two, or three situations:

- *Lack of corroboration (also called nonsubstantiation).* Only one source or evidence item supports one side of the conflict, while multiple independent sources or evidence items support the opposing side. The unsupported information likely is erroneous.

  For example, "An unknown family historian has identified Eleanor as a daughter of James Crow who died in Culpeper County. . . .

Original records do not verify this allegation, which personal, not-for-profit, and commercial Web sites have disseminated." For details, see Thomas W. Jones, "Uncovering Ancestors by Deduction: The Husbands and Parents of Eleanor (née Medley) (Tureman) (Crow) Overton," *National Genealogical Society Quarterly* 94 (December 2006): 287–305, quotation from pp. 288–89.

- *Quality of evidence.* Primary information items from original records support one side of the conflict, while only derivative records, secondary information, or both support the opposing side. The latter qualities, suggesting likelihood of error, tilt the scale toward the primary information items from original records.

  For example, evidence identifying Amzi Leach's father as Benjamin or John Leach was created after his death; evidence suggesting the father was Daniel Wallen comes from original records created by eyewitnesses who knew Amzi's mother and Daniel Wallen.

- *Explanation.* Plausible reasoning explains why evidence items differ. It also justifies discounting evidence supporting one side of a conflict.

  For an example, see the discussion in appendix B (bullet 5 on the article's page 107) of Charles McLain's age in his marriage record.

All three situations may apply to resolving one conflict. When an evidence item is wrong, it often is wrong for two or three reasons. For an example, see figure 6.

Explaining conflict resolutions

We explain in writing the resolution of serious conflicts—especially evidence conflicting with a potential conclusion. Effective explanations of resolved conflicts include three components:

1. Identifying two or more answers in conflict

2. Listing or describing the evidence supporting each side of the conflict

3. Demonstrating that the conflict is resolved by lack of corroboration, quality of evidence, explanation, or a combination

See figure 6 for an example illustrating these three components of a written resolution of conflicting evidence.

Unresolved conflicts

Not all conflicting evidence can be resolved. This might make proof impossible. Stopping short of proof, we may state that a point is unresolved, summarize the related evidence, and explain why the conflict is not resolved.

Figure 6

**Illustration and Analysis of an Explanation of the
Resolution of Conflicting Evidence**

1. The conflicting answers to the question of Charles's parentage are:

- *Charles and Jane E. Jones*
- *C. R. and Virginia Jones*

2. Evidence comes from the lawsuit's case file and a marriage bond (consistent with one answer) and Charles's death certificate (consistent with the other answer). These sources are cited prior to this summary discussion.

The court suit [saying Charles's parents were Charles and Jane E. Jones], as a contemporary legal document dealing with inheritance, merits the greatest credibility. The parties involved in the case were in a position to know the children's parentage. The record was created during Charles Robert's and Virginia's childhood, and their parentage is corroborated by other evidence. The marriage bond posted for Charles Jones to wed Jane E. Jones is evidence only of the parties' intention to marry. Alone, it would not establish his paternity of Jane's subsequent children; but coupled with court testimony on that point, the evidence is convincing. By contrast, the parents alleged for Charles Robert Jones on his death certificate [C. R. and Virginia Jones] are names provided after his death, by a daughter who had no firsthand knowledge of his parents.

3. The bases for the conflict's resolution are:
- The lack of corroboration for the death certificate's information
- The relative qualities of the case file (primary information) and death record (secondary information)
- The explanation that participants in the suit knew Charles's parents

Note: Adapted from Thomas W. Jones, "A Name Switch and a Double-dose of Joneses: Weighing Evidence to Identify Charles R. Jones," *National Genealogical Society Quarterly* 84 (March 1996): 5–16, quoted from p. 16.

We can express a belief that one side of an unresolved conflict is more likely correct. The discussion should make it clear to readers that we are presenting an opinion, not a conclusion from evidence. Recognizing that in such cases we have no conclusion or proof—all we have is a possibility— we qualify the discussion with words like *perhaps* and *possibly*.

Assembling evidence to establish a conclusion

If our thorough research yields either (*1*) only evidence in agreement or (*2*) conflicting evidence we have resolved, we can assemble the evidence into a conclusion. Our options for this assembly range from simple to complex. We use the option that reflects the kind of evidence we have found, the presence or absence of conflicts, and the kinds of evidence on either side of a conflict. Five approaches to assembling evidence are common:

1. *Direct evidence and no conflict.* All applicable evidence items, including at least one direct-evidence item, agree on—are compatible with—a research question's answer. This is the simplest and most common way genealogical evidence appears. Therefore, it is the most common way to assemble genealogical evidence to answer research questions.

   For example, Mary Jones's two marriage records and her parents' family Bible record identify her parents as Silas and Sarah E. (Whiting) Jones. No source—including censuses, Mary's father's and paternal grandfathers' probate records, and Silas and Sarah's marriage record—provides direct, indirect, or negative evidence incompatible with this conclusion.

2. *Resolved conflicting direct evidence.* Two or more direct-evidence items disagree on a research question's answer, the genealogist resolves the disagreement, and all applicable indirect evidence agrees with that resolution.

   For example, Calvin Snell's recorded will says he had a daughter Lydia; other sources name Louisa among his daughters and no Lydia. The conflict is resolved by multiple points of corroboration for Louisa and none for Lydia. For details, see Thomas W. Jones, "The Children of Calvin Snell: Primary versus Secondary Evidence," *National Genealogical Society Quarterly* 83 (March 1995): 17–31.

3. *Resolved conflict between direct evidence and indirect or negative evidence.* One or more direct-evidence items disagree with one or more indirect-evidence or negative-evidence items, and the genealogist resolves the disagreement. The resulting conclusion may arise from either the direct evidence or the indirect or negative evidence.

   For example, a published genealogy says Maxfield Whiting's parents were Henry and Ann (Beverly) Whiting of Gloucester County, Virginia (direct evidence); court records in Stafford and King George counties, Virginia, show—without stating the relationship—that Maxfield's parents were William and Martha (Maxfield) Whiting (indirect evidence). The conflict is resolved by evaluating the sources and information—the direct evidence includes no eyewitness information or documentation; the indirect evidence comes from events, sources, and information for which Maxfield and his mother were creators, informants, or participants. For details, see Thomas W. Jones, "The Parents of Maxfield Whiting of Virginia and Kentucky," *The American Genealogist* 80 (July 2005): 195–200.

4. *Indirect evidence, negative evidence, or a combination of the two; an absence of direct evidence; and no conflict.* No known source answers the research question directly, but the assembled indirect or negative evidence agrees on one answer. This may include relatively rare situations in which all the evidence is negative—information absent from where it might be expected eliminates all but one possible conclusion.

  For example, no source concerning Joseph Dilley who married and paid taxes in Fauquier County, Virginia, in 1804 names his parents, and no record of his proposed father, John Dilley Jr. (implied by a survey of land belonging to John Dilley Sr.) names John's children. Direct evidence is absent, but indirect evidence from tax records and from John's witnessing a deed and the absence of evidence for other candidates (therefore, negative evidence) support John's identification as Joseph's father. No evidence conflicts with this conclusion. For details, see Thomas W. Jones, "Dilley of Northern Virginia and Ohio: A Proposed Solution Hanging on a Single Word," *The American Genealogist* 79 (July 2004): 220–27.

5. *Resolved conflicting indirect evidence, negative evidence, or a combination; and an absence of direct evidence.* No known source answers the research question directly, indirect/negative-evidence items disagree on the answer, and the genealogist resolves the disagreement.

  For example, Philip Pritchett's initiating a lawsuit in Fauquier County implies he lived there (indirect evidence), but the absence of Pritchetts in the county's tax lists around that time (negative evidence) implies he lived elsewhere. The evidence of a Fauquier County residence is unsubstantiated, and indirect evidence shows that plaintiff Philip lived in Fairfax County and previously in Stafford County, thus enabling a documented explanation (along with lack of corroboration for the opposing evidence item) to resolve the conflict. See the article in appendix A, its pages 30–33.

Chapter 6 exercises

1. What is the definition of conflicting evidence?

2. Why does genealogical proof require us to resolve conflicts with a conclusion?

3. Following the model, place in the table below the elements of the following conflict-resolution discussions from the articles in appendixes A and B and circle the likely-correct answer that the conflict resolution supports:

   a. The article in appendix B, paragraph at the top of its page 106 (2 conflicts)

   b. The article in appendix A, the discussion under "Supporting Conclusion 4," on its pages 35–36

   c. The article in appendix A, the discussion under "Supporting Conclusion 6," on its page 37

   d. The article in appendix B, the figure and discussion at the top of its page 112

   e. The article in appendix B, its page 108, the point concerning Charles's mother's name; including the supporting timeline on the article's pages 109–14 and some of the bullet points on its pages 114–16

ONE SIDE OF CONFLICT	OPPOSING SIDE OF CONFLICT	KINDS OF EVIDENCE IN CONFLICT	WAY(S) CONFLICT IS RESOLVED
a1. Charles was born in January 1854 [for the resolution, see page 119]	Charles was born in 1848–49	Direct versus direct	No corroboration for 1848–49; explanation
a2. Emma's husband was not previously married	Emma married Ida's ex-husband	Direct versus indirect	No corroboration; quality of evidence; explanation
b.			
c.			
d.			
e.			

4. Propose and explain a resolution to the following conflicting evidence of Charles Jones's birth date. Mention in your explanation the kind(s) of evidence in conflict and the kind(s) of resolutions you used.

BIRTH-DATE EVIDENCE	SOURCES
1839–40	Federal censuses of 1900, 1910, and 1920
22 September 1841	Charles's wife's family Bible and his pension application, death certificate, and two gravestones
1841–42	Federal census of 1880
After March 1842	March 1856 court case in which Charles was disqualified from testifying because he was under age fourteen; his older sister and two uncles gave evidence in the case
1843–44	Federal censuses of 1850, 1860, and 1870
1843–47	Charles's mother's 1853 letter saying he had started school and could "read and writt [*sic*] very well"
1844–45	1861 enlistment date and family lore that he enlisted at age sixteen

Resolution and explanation:

5. Which of the five methods of assembling evidence listed on this book's pages 77–78 was used to support the conclusion *the widow of Lewis "Pritchart" was Frances*? See the article in appendix A, its pages 35–36, bullet 2, and footnotes 27–29. Explain your answer.

6. Which of the five methods of assembling evidence was used to support the conclusion *the parents of Philip Pritchett who died in Kentucky in 1811–12 were Lewis and Mary (Lattimore) Pritchett of Stafford and Fauquier counties, Virginia*. See appendix A, the entire article. Explain your answer.

7. Which of the five methods of assembling evidence was used to support the conclusion *the parents of Ida Tucker's first husband, Charles D. McLain, were James and Phebe McLain*. See appendix B, the entire article. Explain your answer.

Check your answers at the back of the book.

Chapter 7
GPS Element 5: The Written Conclusion

A proved conclusion's written form depends on where that conclusion fits on a continuum of genealogical proof situations, ranging from extremely straightforward to extremely complex. We use the approach that best fits our evidence and its support for the conclusion we wish to present as proved.

We have assembled our evidence, resolved any conflicts, and established a conclusion. We may believe we have proved that conclusion. Proof exists, however, only in writing. It requires a written and documented fact, statement, or explanation showing why we and consumers of our research should believe a conclusion is proved. It does not need to show *how* we executed the research that led to the conclusion.

Demonstrating proof in writing may be easy or difficult, or it may fall somewhere between these extremes. In the simplest situations source citations make proof self-evident. In contrast, the most complex situations may require many pages of documented explanation, enhanced and clarified with timelines, tables, and illustrations. Such challenging situations, though perhaps more interesting and important, are less common than straightforward proof contexts.

Regardless of a case's simplicity or complexity, its written conclusion—the GPS's fifth element—must reflect the GPS's first three elements:

- *GPS element 1—thorough research.* Source citations may adequately show our research scope. If information beyond what the citations show is needed to show research scope, we add it to our footnotes or narrative.

- *GPS element 2—source citations.* Footnotes attached to our narrative contain citations identifying sources supporting our conclusion.

- *GPS element 3—analysis and correlation of information and evidence.* Source citations may adequately reflect our analysis and correlation. If information beyond what the citations show is needed to demonstrate appropriate analysis and correlation, we add it to our footnotes or narrative.

If evidence offers conflicting answers to our research question, the written conclusion must address not only the GPS's first three elements but also the fourth:

- *GPS element 4—resolution of any evidence conflicting with the conclusion.* If no information or evidence conflicts with our proposed answer to the research question, we bypass this GPS element. If any evidence does conflict with that answer, our written conclusion shows how we resolved the conflict.

A written conclusion's form depends on where that conclusion fits on a continuum of genealogical proof situations, ranging from obviously self-evident to extremely complex. We have three options for presenting a conclusion as proved. We select the option that best fits our evidence and how it supports our conclusion:

- *Proof statement* (a data item or sentence in a broader context)

- *Proof summary* (one or a few pages focused on proof)

- *Proof argument* (several or many pages focused on proof)

Proof statements

A proof statement may be a documented data item or sentence stating or showing a conclusion within a documented genealogical article, chapter, chart, report, table, or other printed or online work. A written conclusion meeting the GPS may be this simple, if direct evidence items from credible sources agree perfectly with the statement and no known source conflicts with it.

A footnote containing at least one or two citations accompanies the item or sentence comprising the proof statement. In the context of a larger documented work, this one footnote may be adequate for genealogical proof—for meeting the GPS—if the citations show six characteristics:

1. They are clear, complete, and accurate.

2. Citations in the footnote, the proof statement's context, or both identify at least two independent sources, each specifying the conclusion.

3. They cite sources that competent genealogists would consult to support the conclusion. (For example, if the statement concerns a marriage, one citation might reference the original marriage record containing an eyewitness account.)

4. They cite at least one original record that supports the conclusion.

5. They refer to at least one primary information item used as direct, indirect, or negative evidence of the conclusion.

6. They cite no authored work, derivative record, or secondary information that could be replaced by a corresponding original record or primary information.

When citations with these characteristics accompany proof statements in a larger documented context, the proof statement may meet four GPS elements:

- Citations in the single footnote and the proof statement's context will reflect GPS elements 2 (clear and accurate source citations) and 3 (analysis and correlation of evidence).

- Citations within the work containing the proof statement will show the research scope, demonstrating GPS element 1 (reasonably exhaustive research). They also are likely to add support to the proof statement.

- The proof statement itself will demonstrate GPS element 5 (clearly written conclusion).

Proof statements cannot handle GPS element 4—resolution of conflicting evidence. Resolution of conflicting evidence requires explanation—more than a single documented data item or statement. Consequently, if evidence conflicts with our proposed conclusion, our written explanation must be in the form of a proof summary or proof argument, not a proof statement.

Table 8 shows seven related proof statements meeting the GPS. Although some of the five footnotes do not contain two citations, their context

---

Table 8

Seven Related Proof Statements in Context

> Three days later, in Kansas City, Missouri, "Miss Clara D. Kinaman" of Sedgwick County, Kansas—just north of Sumner—married Richard Y. Ford.[33] In 1887–88 and 1892 the Fords lived in Wichita, in Sedgwick County.[34] Ford's "habitual drunkenness" caused Clara to leave him in November 1892 and return to Conway Springs. On 30 November 1894 she filed for divorce, granted on 23 January 1896.[35] In 1898 Clara Ford, "wid. [of] Richard," resided in Kansas City, Missouri.[36] Quite alive, Richard was treated for the "liquor habit" in Wichita in 1901. He died, apparently childless, in Pittsburg, Kansas, on 9 March 1909.[37]

> 33. Jackson Co., Mo., Marriage Record 7:463, Ford-Kinnaman; Recorder of Deeds, Kansas City, Mo.; FHL microfilm 1,016,666. For Ford's first name, see *Annual Directory of the City of Wichita* (Wichita: F. A. North, 1888), 170.
> 34. *Annual Directory of the City of Wichita* (1887), 139; (1888), 170; and (1892), 132.
> 35. Clara D. Ford, Petition, 30 November 1894; Sumner Co., case file no. 8124, Ford v. Ford.
> 36. *Hoye's City Directory of Kansas City, Mo.* (Kansas City: Hoye, 1898), 271, for "Ford Clara D wid Richard r 1424 Grand av." Also, "Death of a Pioneer," *Quincy Daily Herald*, 4 November 1898, page 1, col. 2. Adam was "survived by his wife and two daughters, one in Colorado and the other in Kansas City."
> 37. "He Was Rescued," *Wichita City Eagle*, 15 May 1901, page 2, col. 6. Also, "Dick Ford Dead," *Pittsburg Headlight*, evening edition, Pittsburg, Kans., 8 March 1909, sixth unnumbered page, col. 3. The author thanks Evie Bresette, CG, for research on Richard Ford.

Note: Excerpted from Thomas W. Jones, "Misleading Records Debunked: The Surprising Case of George Wellington Edison Jr.," *National Genealogical Society Quarterly* 100 (June 2012): 133–56 at p. 138.

contains corroborating documentation for each statement. For example, the divorce file corroborates the marriage. The last footnote documents the extract's last two statements.

Proof summaries

Proof summaries are documented lists or narratives stating facts that support or lead to a proved conclusion. Unlike proof statements, which require a broader context, proof summaries may stand alone. A proof summary might, for example, comprise a report for a client or personal files, or it might accompany a lineage-society application. Proof summaries also, however, may appear as parts of articles, blogs, case studies, chapters, reports, and other documented genealogical works.

A combination of two circumstances indicates when a proof summary is the best choice for a written conclusion meeting the GPS:

- The written conclusion requires more than one documented fact or statement and footnote to explain the conclusion and show the documentation supporting it.

- The written conclusion does not involve a complicated question of identity or difficult-to-resolve conflicting evidence, enabling the genealogist to fully explain the rationale for proof, including the resolution of any conflicting evidence, within a few paragraphs or pages.

Footnotes accompanying a proof summary cite all the sources supporting or documenting the conclusion. Effective citations will collectively show eight characteristics:

1. They are clear, complete, and accurate.

2. They show that the genealogist bypassed no likely relevant source.

3. They document all statements.

4. They cite at least two independent sources supporting the conclusion.

5. They cite all the sources that competent genealogists would consult to support the conclusion.

6. They cite at least one original record providing information that directly, indirectly, or negatively supports the conclusion.

7. They refer to at least one primary information item used directly, indirectly, or negatively as evidence of the conclusion.

8. They cite no authored work, derivative source, or secondary information that could be replaced by a corresponding original record and primary information.

When citations with these characteristics accompany a proof summary it will meet all five GPS elements:

- The proof summary's citations will reflect GPS elements 1 (thorough research) and 2 (clear and accurate source citations).

- Those citations will at least partially demonstrate GPS element 3 (analysis and correlation of evidence). Explanations within the proof summary's paragraphs or list items may further reflect GPS element 3.

- If evidence conflicts with the conclusion, the proof summary's paragraphs or list items will address GPS element 4 (explanation of the resolution of conflicting evidence).

- The proof summary itself will demonstrate GPS element 5 (clearly written conclusion).

Proof summaries typically begin or end with a statement of the conclusion being proved:

- If we state the conclusion first, we enumerate the points explaining why we consider that conclusion proved. This may be a list, likely with a footnote attached to each list item. Alternatively, we may provide the explanation in a documented narrative format.

- If we end with a statement of the conclusion, we begin with the research question. We continue with a list or narrative to develop the rationale for a proved answer.

Table 5 (under chapter 5) shows a proof summary in a list format with the conclusion stated first. For proof summaries in a narrative format, see the article in appendix A. Each of the seven "Supporting Conclusion" sections is a proof summary in narrative format, enhanced with lists, tables, and figures. (The entire article, however, is a proof argument.)

Proof arguments

Proof arguments are documented narratives in which genealogists explain why the answer to a complex genealogical problem should be considered proved. Proof arguments may be stand-alone documents, like articles, case studies, reports, and monographs, or they could be part of a chapter, family history, report, or other documented genealogical work.

Differences between proof arguments and proof summaries

Proof summaries and arguments represent a division between two parts of a continuum:

- We use *proof summaries* for less complex cases, those where questions of identity and conflicting evidence can be resolved without serious difficulty. These cases usually can be explained in a few pages or less. Proof summaries typically overarch proof statements, which, when combined, support the case for proof.

- We use *proof arguments* for more complex cases, those where questions of identity or conflicting evidence are difficult to resolve. They usually require more than a few pages of explanation. Proof arguments typically overarch proof statements and proof summaries, which, when combined, support the case for proof.

Like proof summaries, proof arguments are thoroughly documented. Citations for proof arguments should show the same eight characteristics as those for proof summaries. Proof arguments also demonstrate the GPS's five elements in the same way as proof summaries.

Divisions within proof arguments

Proof arguments typically have three major sections:

- *Beginning.* More than an introduction, the argument's opening section explains the research question, identifies the starting-point persons of interest, and describes any relevant contextual information, including prior research on the same family or question and challenges related to the geographic area, time period, family, or other factors. Depending on the best choice for unfolding the proof argument, the genealogist might state the proved conclusion in the proof argument's beginning. For an example, see the first five pages of the article in appendix B.

- *Middle.* The proof argument's longest section describes the rationale for proof. It lays out the evidence, interprets it, resolves conflicting evidence, and explains why the resulting evidence composite supports the conclusion. The argument's middle section may use charts, figures (including maps), lists (including timelines), and tables to present the research results and demonstrate patterns within them. This section leads up to and states or restates the conclusion—the answer to the research question presented in the argument's opening section.

- *End.* The proof argument's shortest section briefly recapitulates the main points showing the conclusion is proved. It may restate the conclusion and place it in relevant historical, genealogical, methodological, or other contexts. For an example, see the last three pages of the article in appendix B.

Developing the argument

Some approaches to organizing a proof argument's middle section may be ineffective or hard to follow. We should avoid, for example, writing about the sequence in which we undertook the research. We also should avoid grouping by source categories (first the census data, then the deed data, and so forth). Instead, the argument should unfold logically, in a sequence designed to explain—one point at a time—the rationale for considering the conclusion proved.

The organization of a proof argument's middle section depends on how we conceptualize each problem, what relevant evidence shows, and the clearest, most efficient way to explain the conclusion. Those circumstances, not preference, guide our choice. Four approaches are common, and proof arguments often incorporate more than one or all of them:

- *Single hypothesis.* We state the conclusion and discuss its supporting evidence.

- *Alternative hypotheses.* We propose two or more competing hypothetical answers to a research question and discuss the evidence for each hypothesis, pro and con, convincingly eliminating all the hypotheses but one, the last to be discussed.

- *Building blocks.* We organize the argument around the points supporting the conclusion. Proceeding from what was initially known about the research subject, we finish with the answer to the research question. We sequence the points so each builds on the one before, with little or no backtracking, repetition, or cross-referencing. If the points are independent, we begin with the major points and end with the minor points.

- *Syllogisms.* "If-then" statements are syllogisms—for example, *if Minerva Tucker's brothers were* Pierces, *then Minerva's maiden name was* Pierce. A syllogism's "if" portion is a "proposition," and its "then" portion is a "premise." Many genealogical conclusions involve syllogisms, often a series of them, one leading to the next. Sometimes genealogists' syllogisms are complex, with several premises establishing one proposition or containing some negative premises ("if no Moses Fox paid taxes in 1803 and Moses Fox sold land in 1804, then. . . ." We may organize a proof argument's middle portion following a sequence of syllogisms, propositions, or premises, building up to the conclusion that all the syllogisms support.

Like many complex proof arguments, the article in appendix A uses all four approaches:

- Its overall structure is that of a *single hypothesis.* The top of the article's third page states the hypothesis that Philip's parents were Lewis and Mary (Lattimore) Pritchett. The article then establishes the points supporting that relationship as a proved conclusion.

- The top half of the article's last page considers three *alternative hypotheses* for Philip's parents, and it then eliminates two of them.

- The article uses *building blocks* organization to present and discuss the data. Each of its seven "Supporting Conclusion" sections represents a major point or building block. One leads to the next and eventually to the answer to the research question "Who were Philip's parents?"

- Several of the article's sections use *syllogisms.* For example, if Philip lived in Fairfax County, he was related to Lewis; if Lewis came from Stafford County, so did Philip; and if Philip was not the Fairfax County Lewis's son, he was someone else's son.

Clear writing

Proof statements, summaries, and arguments are "clearly written." Clear writing for proof statements, summaries, and arguments includes twelve points concerning words, sentences, paragraphs, overall structure, and tone:

- We choose words that communicate precisely what we mean. We avoid vague and needless words.

- Our sentences are well formed, grammatical, and direct. Varying in length, they avoid complex structures, trite expressions, mismatches or confusion between pronouns and the nouns they refer back to, and unnecessary passive-voice constructions.

- Present-tense verbs refer to extant sources and living people. Past-tense verbs refer to no-longer-extant materials and deceased people. (Consequently, much genealogical writing is in the past tense.)

- Where possible, we avoid using complicated tenses and mixing tenses within a sentence or paragraph.

- Our narrative focuses on our research subjects and the evidence of their lives and relationships—they are the subjects of most of our sentences. We discuss sources to a lesser extent, because most information about sources belongs in the citations and footnotes.

- Letting the evidence speak for itself, we keep ourselves in the background.

- We avoid digressions—points that do not advance our case for proof.

- We do not speculate about possibilities lacking adequate evidence.

- We arrange narrative proof summaries and proof arguments in paragraphs with topic sentences. The paragraphs are neither too long nor too short—typically more than two sentences and less than a page.

- Transitions move the narrative from one paragraph or section to the next. Besides wording, transitions often include subheadings reflecting the essay's outline and "announcing" changes in focus.

- The tone of a proof argument or summary is that of a "defense" in the academic sense. We write to show readers that a conclusion is proved.

- The genre is more that of technical writing—precise, objective, and focused—than that of literary writing, which may be more descriptive, personal, subjective, and wide ranging.

A persuasive tone and technical-writing style may be consistent within articles, case studies, and reports that consist mostly of a proof summary or argument. Tone and style may vary, however, in narrative biographies and family histories, which often include proof summaries and arguments, especially when an identity or relationship is not self-evident. Segments that establish proof will be more precise and persuasive than segments describing people, activities, and events.

Chapter 7 exercises

1. Locate three proof statements in the article in appendix A. State the conclusion that each statement proves.

2. Locate two proof summaries in the article in appendix A. State the conclusion that each summary proves.

3. Describe the "beginning" of the proof-argument article in appendix A.

4. Describe the "end" of the proof-argument article in appendix A.

5. List two approaches the author of the proof-argument article in appendix B uses to develop the argument's "middle." Explain or give an example of each.

6. Select a genealogical article of interest to you that you believe is a proof argument. [Via the NGS website's members-only area, NGS members may download *NGS Quarterly* articles back through 1979; everyone will find a short selection of genealogical articles and proof arguments online at "Sample Work Products," *Board for Certification of Genealogists* (http://www.bcgcertification.org/skillbuilders/worksamples.html). You also may select articles from elsewhere.] Use your selected article to respond to the following:

   a.   State or summarize the main conclusion that your selection proves.

b.   Locate three proof *statements* in your selection. State or summarize the conclusion that each statement proves.

c.   Locate at least one proof *summary* in your selection. State or summarize the conclusion that each located proof summary proves.

d.   Describe the division between your selection's "beginning" and its "middle."

e.   Describe the division between your selected proof argument's "middle" and its "end."

f.   List one or more approaches the proof argument's author uses to develop the argument's "middle." Describe or give an example of each.

g.   Use this chapter's criteria for "Clear writing" (pages 90–91) to explain why or why not the selected proof argument is "clearly written."

Check your answers at the back of the book.

Chapter 8

Using the GPS

*Not only do we strive to produce work that meets the GPS, we use it
to evaluate other genealogists' conclusions.*

Yes answers to eleven questions about a genealogical conclusion—whether
our own or another genealogists'—and its context will indicate the conclusion meets the GPS:

a. Does the writer state a clear research question—what is it?

b. Do the writer's citations address sources likely to help answer that
question?

c. Do the citations reflect a search that was reasonably (not necessarily
perfectly) thorough?

d. Do the citations in conjunction with the text indicate that all or most
sources are likely reliable?

e. If the conclusion rests on any error-prone sources or information,
does the writer justify their use?

f. Do the footnotes, or footnotes and text, show that the writer analyzed
all the supporting sources?

g. Does the writer base the conclusion on the correlation of evidence
from all relevant sources?

h. If the conclusion is not self-evident, does the writer present correlations in narrative, list, table, map, or other form?

i. Does the writer convincingly resolve all conflicts with evidence supporting the conclusion?

j. Does the writer state the conclusion clearly?

k. Does the author convincingly show or explain why the conclusion is
correct?

When assessing our own work, a *no* answer to even one of the above questions means our conclusion is not proved. More work remains. Addressing
a *no* answer may be simple (restating the conclusion, for example), difficult (extending the research, for example), or somewhere between these
extremes.

A *no* answer in an assessment of another genealogist's work suggests caution. Trusting the work, building on it, or incorporating it into our work could needlessly introduce error. We might opt to address the deficiency, use the work as a finding aid for our own research, or bypass it completely.

Chapter 8 exercises

1. Select a book of interest to you that purports to accurately present family relationships from the past. Select a conclusion that the work's author seems to believe is proved, and answer the following eleven questions about that conclusion, its context, and its presentation. *Yes* answers to all eleven questions will indicate the conclusion meets the GPS:

   a. Does the writer state a clear research question?

      If *yes*, what is the research question?

   b. Do the writer's citations address sources likely to help answer that question?

   c. Do the citations reflect a search that was reasonably (not necessarily perfectly) thorough?

   d. Do the citations in conjunction with the text indicate that all or most sources are likely reliable?

   e. If the conclusion rests on any error-prone sources or information, does the writer justify their use?

   f. Do the footnotes, or footnotes and text, show that the writer analyzed all the supporting sources?

   g. Does the writer base the conclusion on the correlation of evidence from all relevant sources?

   h. If the conclusion is not self-evident, does the writer present correlations in narrative, list, table, map, or other form?

   i. Does the writer convincingly resolve all conflicts with evidence supporting the conclusion?

   j. Does the writer state the conclusion clearly?

    k.   Does the author convincingly show or explain why the conclusion is correct?

2. Select a website of interest to you that purports to accurately present family relationships from the past. Select a conclusion that the work's author seems to believe is proved, and answer the following eleven questions about that conclusion, its context, and its presentation. *Yes* answers to all eleven questions will indicate the conclusion meets the GPS:

    a.   Does the writer state a clear research question?

           If *yes*, what is the research question?

    b.   Do the writer's citations address sources likely to help answer that question?

    c.   Do the citations reflect a search that was reasonably (not necessarily perfectly) thorough?

    d.   Do the citations in conjunction with the text indicate that all or most sources are likely reliable?

    e.   If the conclusion rests on any error-prone sources or information, does the writer justify their use?

    f.   Do the footnotes, or footnotes and text, show that the writer analyzed all the supporting sources?

    g.   Does the writer base the conclusion on the correlation of evidence from all relevant sources?

    h.   If the conclusion is not self-evident, does the writer present correlations in narrative, list, table, map, or other form?

    i.   Does the writer convincingly resolve all conflicts with evidence supporting the conclusion?

    j.   Does the writer state the conclusion clearly?

    k.   Does the author convincingly show or explain why the conclusion is correct?

3. Select a journal article of interest to you that purports to accurately present family relationships from the past. Select a conclusion that the work's author seems to believe is proved, and answer the following eleven questions about that conclusion, its context, and its presentation. *Yes* answers to all eleven questions will indicate the conclusion meets the GPS:

   a.   Does the writer state a clear research question?

        If *yes*, what is the research question?

   b.   Do the writer's citations address sources likely to help answer that question?

   c.   Do the citations reflect a search that was reasonably (not necessarily perfectly) thorough?

   d.   Do the citations in conjunction with the text indicate that all or most sources are likely reliable?

   e.   If the conclusion rests on any error-prone sources or information, does the writer justify their use?

   f.   Do the footnotes, or footnotes and text, show that the writer analyzed all the supporting sources?

   g.   Does the writer base the conclusion on the correlation of evidence from all relevant sources?

   h.   If the conclusion is not self-evident, does the writer present correlations in narrative, list, table, map, or other form?

   i.   Does the writer convincingly resolve all conflicts with evidence supporting the conclusion?

   j.   Does the writer state the conclusion clearly?

   k.   Does the author convincingly show or explain why the conclusion is correct?

4. Select a conclusion from your own research that you believe is proved, and answer the following eleven questions about that conclusion, its context, and its presentation. *Yes* answers to the eleven questions will indicate the conclusion meets the GPS:

    a.   Does the writer state a clear research question?

           If *yes*, what is the research question?

    b.   Do the writer's citations address sources likely to help answer that question?

    c.   Do the citations reflect a search that was reasonably (not necessarily perfectly) thorough?

    d.   Do the citations in conjunction with the text indicate that all or most sources are likely reliable?

    e.   If the conclusion rests on any error-prone sources or information, does the writer justify their use?

    f.   Do the footnotes, or footnotes and text, show that the writer analyzed all the supporting sources?

    g.   Does the writer base the conclusion on the correlation of evidence from all relevant sources?

    h.   If the conclusion is not self-evident, does the writer present correlations in narrative, list, table, map, or other form?

    i.   Does the writer convincingly resolve all conflicts with evidence supporting the conclusion?

    j.   Does the writer state the conclusion clearly?

    k.   Does the author convincingly show or explain why the conclusion is correct?

Answers to chapter 8 exercises will vary with the material you select.

Chapter 9

Conclusion

As you repeatedly apply the discipline of focused and systematic genealogical research, reasoning, and writing, you will find yourself becoming more and more proficient.

In this book you have learned much about the genealogy field's standard for differentiating acceptable conclusions from those that fall short of acceptability—the Genealogical Proof Standard (GPS) and its five elements. Your learning includes the value of starting with focused research questions and how to craft effective research questions. You have applied the standard's fundamental concepts: (*a*) sources are authored works or original or derivative records; (*b*) information may be primary, secondary, or indeterminable; and (*c*) evidence may be direct, indirect, or negative. You also have learned how to plan research to answer your research questions and how to evaluate whether or not that research was "reasonably exhaustive." You have learned the fundamentals of citing the sources you have consulted, how to use tests of analysis and correlation to assess the evidence your sources contain, and how to resolve conflicting evidence, assemble evidence to form a conclusion, and present that conclusion as a documented proof statement, summary, or argument. You also have learned how to use the GPS to evaluate other genealogists' work to minimize the risk of polluting your research with their incorrect conclusions.

To continue learning consult works listed in this book's "Reading and Source List." Study examples of how other researchers assemble evidence and present and defend their cases for genealogical proof. You will find many examples cited throughout this book, in every issue of the *National Genealogical Society Quarterly*, and in similar publications.

More important, plan and execute your own research on a focused genealogical question that interests you. Test the evidence you gather; assemble it into a conclusion; defend it with a written proof statement, argument, or summary; and present it to others.

As you repeatedly apply the discipline of focused and systematic genealogical research, documentation, reasoning, and writing, you will find yourself becoming more and more proficient. You will develop the ability to solve difficult problems and present them in ways that will make sense to others. You will reconstruct identities and relationships that you cannot see, but you will portray those reconstructions accurately. You will have resurrected long-forgotten history and reliably advanced your own, your family's, and other genealogists' knowledge of the past, helping us understand the present. Your work will be of value for future generations to appreciate and to build upon.

Appendix A

Pritchett Article

Logic Reveals the Parents of
Philip Pritchett of Virginia and Kentucky

By Thomas W. Jones, Ph.D., CG, CGL, FASG

*No sole source even implies the relationship. Instead, when
evidence from many sources is correlated, they collectively point
to a conclusion. A reasoning process confirms the kinship.*

When no record names a man's parents, evidence-based reasoning may determine his parentage. If the result meets standards for genealogical proof, confidence in its accuracy can be high. Such was the case of Philip Pritchett, a Kentuckian who left no known record of parents or origins.[1]

A VIRGINIAN IN KENTUCKY

Philip "Pritchartt" died in Montgomery County, Kentucky, between 10 November 1811 and 10 March 1812, the signing and proving of his will. Naming "Alpherd" and Lewis among "all my children," he designated his wife Hannah and William Kemper executors.[2] Philip was born before 1764–65.[3] He paid taxes in Clark County in 1795–96 and in Montgomery County in 1797–1809.[4]

© Thomas W. Jones, Ph.D., CG, CGL, FASG; 9232 Arlington Blvd.; Fairfax, VA 22031-2505; Tom@JonesResearchServices.com. Dr. Jones, one of the *NGS Quarterly's* two lead editors, works as a genealogical researcher, editor, and educator. Melinde Lutz Sanborn, FASG, edited this piece. The research reported in this article was commissioned by Carl D. Pritchett, who gives permission for its publication. Deb Cyprych conducted part of the research's Kentucky phase.

1. Unless quoting original records, this paper will spell the surname as Pritchett.
2. Montgomery Co., Ky., Will Book A:106–7, Philip Pritchartt; County Court, Mount Sterling, Ky.; microfilm 252,360, Family History Library (FHL), Salt Lake City.
3. 1810 U.S. census, Montgomery Co., Ky., p. 377, Philip Pritchet; National Archives and Records Administration (NARA) microfilm publication M252, roll 7. Philip was over age forty-five. The 1800 census of Kentucky does not survive.
4. Kentucky Tax Assessor, Tax Books, Clark Co., 1793–1797, 1799–1809, for Philip Pritchet (1795, 6:25) and Phill Prichard (1796, 2:21); Kentucky Historical Society; FHL microfilm 7,930. Kentucky Tax Assessor, Tax Books, Montgomery Co., 1797 and 1799–1810, for Philip Pritchett (1797, William Thompson's district, p. 37), Phillip Prichard (1799, p. 23), Phillip Pritchard (1800, Jesse Woodroof's district, p. 24), Philip Prichard (1801, p. 36), Philip Pritchett (1802, first list, p. 15), Philip Pritchet (1803, 2:32), Philip Pritchett (1804, 2:31, and 1805, 1:28), Philip Pritchet (1806, second book, p. 27), Philip Pritchett (1807, first book, p. 31, and 1808, 2:24), and Philip Pritchard (1809, first book, p. 28); Kentucky Historical Society, Frankfort; FHL microfilm 8,168. The 1798 book is missing.

NATIONAL GENEALOGICAL SOCIETY QUARTERLY 97 (MARCH 2009): 29–38

30   *National Genealogical Society Quarterly*

Contemporary Pritchetts in both counties—Jesse, John Junior, John Senior, and Willis—may have been his relatives.[5]

In Fauquier County, Virginia, in September 1783 Philip "Pritchard" sued Moses Baker for trespass, assault, and battery. "Lewis Pritchard his next friend" represented Philip, a minor.[6] The young plaintiff's uncommon name and several parallels identify him as Philip Pritchett who appeared in Kentucky twelve years later:

- William Kemper, Philip's executor in Kentucky, had lived in Fauquier County and reportedly was born there.[7]
- Philip's son Lewis had the same name as the representative in the lawsuit.
- The Virginian's status as a minor in 1783 is consistent with the Kentuckian's age in 1810. Together they narrow Philip's birth to between September 1762 and 6 August 1765.[8]

Although Philip sued in Fauquier County, he apparently never lived there while an adult, complicating the search for his parents. Further hurdles included record losses in Virginia counties where he did live, several contemporary Lewis and Philip Pritchetts, and infrequent Pritchett land ownership. Perhaps for these reasons, published sources have garbled the family's relationships.

---

5. Kentucky Tax Assessor, Tax Books, Clark Co., 1795–96, for John Pritchet (1795, Joseph Smith's district, p. 10), John Prichett (1796, Micajah Harrison's book, p. 29), and "Willias" Prichett (1796, Micajah Harrison's book, p. 30). Also, Kentucky Tax Assessor, Tax Books, Montgomery Co., 1797 and 1799–1810, for Jesse Pritchett (1804, 1:15), Jesse Prichet (1805, 3:19), Jesse Prichett (1806, first book, p. 22), Jesse Pritchett (1807, second book, p. 18), "Jeses" Pritchet (1808, first book, p. 24), and Jesse Pritchette (1809, 2:23); also, Jn° Pritchett (1797, William Thompson's district, p. 37), John Prichard (1799, p. 25), John Prichett (1800, William Ellis's district, p. 19), John Prichard (1801, p. 37), John Pritchett, (1802, second book, p. 13, and 1803, 1:14 and 3:24), John Pritchett and John Pritchett Sen[r]. (1804, 1:22), John Prichet Jr. and John Prichet Senr. (1805, 3:19), John Prichett (1806, first book, p. 21), John Pritchett and John Pritchett Jun[r] (1807, second book, p. 18), John Pritchet "Juni" and John Pritchet "Sen" (1808, first book, pp. 24–25, respectively), and John Pritchette "Senr" and John Pritchette (1809, 2:23); also, Willis Pritchett (1802, first list, p. 15), Willis Pritchet (1803, 3:24), Willis Pritchett (1804, 1:15; 1806, first book, p. 21), and Willis Pritchette (1809, 2:23).

6. Fauquier Co., Minute Book, 1781–84, p. 192, Pritchard v. Baker; County Court, Warrenton, Va.; Fauquier Co. microfilm 47, Library of Virginia (LVA), Richmond. The case was "Discontinued being agreed by the parties."

7. Virginia Auditor of Public Accounts, Personal Property Tax Lists, Fauquier Co., 1782–96, for William Kemper (1787, list B, unpaginated; 1789, list A, p. 16; 1790, list B, p. 14; 1792, list B, p. 14; 1793, list B, p. 15; and 1794, list B, unpaginated); manuscript collections, LVA; LVA Personal Property Tax Books microfilm 110. In 1787 William was sixteen to twenty-one years old, and John Kemper was responsible for his tax. For William's reported birthplace, see Willis M. Kemper, *Genealogy of the Kemper Family: Descendants of John Kemper of Virginia . . .* (Chicago: Geo. K. Hazlitt, 1899), 79.

8. The first date is twenty-one years before Philip's court appearance as a minor. The second is forty-five years before the 1810 census enumeration date. For the latter see Anne Brunner Eales and Robert M. Kvasnicka, *Guide to Genealogical Research in the National Archives of the United States* (Washington, D.C.: National Archives and Records Administration, 2000), 23.

DETERMINING PHILIP'S PARENTAGE

Despite research challenges, Philip's parents can be identified as Lewis and Mary (née Lattimore) Pritchett. No record of Philip names his parents, and no record of Lewis and Mary identifies Philip as their son. While no sole source even implies their relationship, evidence correlated from many sources establishes it. Seven supporting conclusions corroborate the identity of Philip's parents.

Supporting Conclusion 1: Philip Lived in Fairfax County

In 1787 apparently the only white male Virginian over age sixteen named Philip Pritchett (or any variant) lived in Fairfax County.[9] He paid taxes there from 1786 through 1793.[10] Besides his name's uniqueness in 1787, four points imply this Fairfax County man had been the 1783 Fauquier County plaintiff:

1. Fairfax County lies about ten miles east of Fauquier County. See figure 1.
2. Lewis Pritchett, of the same name as Philip's next friend in 1783, was the only other Pritchett taxpayer living in Fairfax County from 1782 through 1801.[11]
3. Lewis and Philip may have been overseer tenants on the same estate. In 1787 they were assessed for different portions of John Gibson's slaves and livestock, and Gibson was charged with the tax.[12]
4. Although Philip sued in Fauquier County in 1783, no Pritchett paid Fauquier County taxes from 1782 (the first year for these taxes) through at least 1787.[13]

9. Netti Schreiner-Yantis and Florene Speakman Love, *The 1787 Census of Virginia: An Accounting of the Name of Every White Male Tithable Over 21 Years; the Number of White Males between 16 and 21 Years; the Number of Slaves Over 16 and those Under 16 Years; together with a Listing of their Horses, Cattle and Carriages; and also the Names of all Persons to whom Ordinary Licenses and Physician's Licenses were Issued*, 3 vols. (Springfield, Va.: Genealogical Books in Print, 1987), 2:1063, 2:1067, and 3:1859–61. The compilers describe the work as identifying "between 95% and 98% of all white male tithables" in Virginia. See 1:xi.

10. Virginia Auditor of Public Accounts, Personal Property Tax Lists, Fairfax County, 1780–1790A and 1790B–1809A, for Philip Pritchard (1786, William Deneal's list, unpaginated), Philip Pritchart (1787, Martin Cockburn's district, unpaginated), Phillip Prichert (1788, James Wren's district, p. 6), Phillip Pritchart (1789, James Wren's district, p. 16), Phillip Pritchett (1790, James Wren's district, p. 11), and Phillip Pritchard (1791, James Wren's district, p. 10; 1792, James Wren's district, p. 11; and 1793, Truro Parish, unpaginated); LVA manuscript collections; LVA personal property tax microfilm reels 106–7.

11. Ibid., for Lewis Pritchard (1782, unpaginated; 1783, Alexander Henderson's list, p. 2; 1784, Richard Chichester's district, his list 2 taken by Ed Payne, unpaginated), [illegible first name] Pritchett (1785, William Payne's list, Truro Parish, unpaginated), Lewis Pritchard (1786, William Deneal's list, unpaginated), Lewis Pritcher (1787, Martin Cockburn's district, unpaginated; 1788, James Wren's district, page 12), Lewis Pritchard (1789, James Wren's district, p. 15), Lewis Pritchett (James Wren's district, p. 11), Lewis Pritchard (1791, James Wren's district, p. 10; 1792, James Wren's district, p. 11; 1793, Truro Parish, unpaginated; 1794, p. 12), Lewis Pritchart (1795, p. 13), Lewis Prichard (1796, George Summers's district, p. 10), Lewis Pritcherd (1797, Thomas Pollard's district, p. 18), Lewis Pritchard (1800, Thomas Pollard Junr.'s district, p. 13), and Lewis Pritchart (1801, Robert Moss's district, p. 12). The lists begin in 1782. "P" sections of the 1798 and 1799 lists are illegible.

12. Ibid., for Lewis Pritchert and Philip Pritchart (1787, Martin Cockburn's district, unpaginated).

13. Virginia Auditor of Public Accounts, Personal Property Tax Lists, Fauquier County, 1780–96.

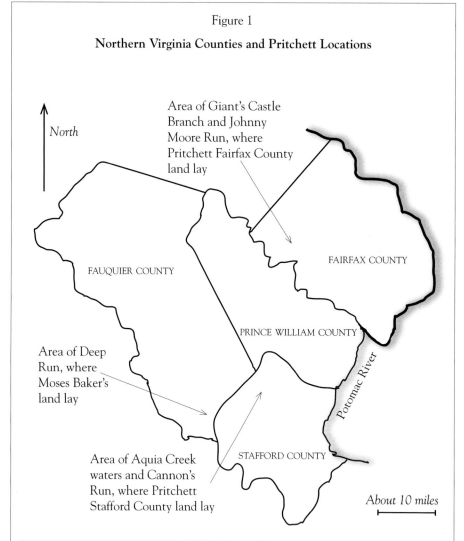

32   *National Genealogical Society Quarterly*

Figure 1

Northern Virginia Counties and Pritchett Locations

Area of Giant's Castle
Branch and Johnny
Moore Run, where
Pritchett Fairfax County
land lay

North

FAIRFAX COUNTY

FAUQUIER COUNTY

PRINCE WILLIAM COUNTY

Area of Deep
Run, where
Moses Baker's
land lay

Potomac River

Area of Aquia Creek
waters and Cannon's
Run, where Pritchett
Stafford County land lay

STAFFORD COUNTY

About 10 miles

 Notes: For Baker's land, see Fauquier Co., Deed Book 8:179–81, Butler to Baker (1784); County Court, Warrenton, Va.; Fauquier Co. microfilm 4, Library of Virginia (LVA), Richmond. For Pritchett land on waters of Aquia Creek, see Stafford Co., Deed Book S:25 and 37, Philips to Edrington (1780); S:40–43, Hansbrough to Murphy (1780); and S:331–32, Pritchett to Wood (1785); all at County Court, Stafford, Va., and on LVA Stafford Co. microfilm 1. For Pritchett land on Cannon's Run, see Stafford Co., Deed Book MM:338, Connor to Heflin (1841); LVA Stafford Co. microfilm 3. For Pritchett Fairfax County land, see Fairfax Co., Deed Books S1:136, Pollard to Philip Pritchard, land on Giant's Castle Branch (now Castle Creek) (1790); and B2:511, Turley to Lewis Pritchart, land on "Johnamore" Run (1800); both at Circuit Court Archives, Fairfax, Va. For the watercourses' locations, see *County Road Map Atlas* (Richmond: Commonwealth of Virginia Department of Transportation, 2004), 29i (Fairfax Co. detail), 30 (Fauquier Co.), and 89a (Stafford Co. detail). Map drawn by author.

The Parents of Philip Pritchett of Virginia and Kentucky   33

Chronology agrees with the Fairfax County Philip's having been the Fauquier County trespass complainant. His first listing, in 1786, as a Fairfax County taxpayer above age twenty suggests he was born about 1765.[14] If he avoided paying taxes in his early twenties, he was born a few years earlier. In any case, becoming a taxpayer in 1786 means he would have been a minor in 1783 but old enough to be a victim of trespass, assault, and battery.

Records besides tax lists suggest Philip lived continuously in Fairfax County for several years. In 1788 he was defendant in another trespass suit.[15] In 1790 he was a chain carrier for a survey of John Gibson's land.[16] That same year Philip leased one hundred acres in Fairfax County.[17] The county ordered him and other citizens to repair roads in 1789, 1791, and 1797.[18] (Apparently the county road authorities did not know Philip had stopped paying Fairfax County taxes after 1793 and moved to Kentucky by 1795.)

Philip's 1786 tax-list appearance is consistent with his age above forty-five in Kentucky in 1810. His last paying Fairfax County taxes in 1793 and appearing in Kentucky in 1795 reinforce the conclusion that the Kentuckian had been the minor who sued Moses Baker in Fauquier County in 1783.

Four points indicate a close relationship between Philip and Lewis Pritchett in Fairfax County:

1. They shared responsibility for John Gibson's property in 1787.
2. Philip had a son Lewis.
3. Lewis's name appears as Philip's "next friend" in his 1782 lawsuit.
4. Lewis purchased land in Fairfax County near the property Philip leased in 1790. See figure 1.

Supporting Conclusion 2: Lewis's Stafford County Origins

In 1782 and 1783 two Lewis Pritchetts owned land in Stafford County, Virginia, which lies about ten miles below Fairfax County. See table 1.

In 1780 Lewis Pritchett owned land "on branches of Aquia Run."[19] On 14 November 1785 Lewis and his wife Jane of Stafford County sold the property, one hundred acres "on branch of Aquia." Lewis had bought it from Marias

---

14. Virginia Auditor of Public Accounts, Personal Property Tax Lists, Fairfax County, 1786, for Philip Pritchard (William Deneal's list, unpaginated).

15. Fairfax Co., Order Book 1788–92, pp. 90, 111, 143, and 343, John Dalgarn v. Richard Simpson, Presley Simpson, and Philip Pritchard; Circuit Court Archives, Fairfax, Va. A jury found Philip innocent and the Simpsons guilty of trespass with assault and false imprisonment.

16. Fairfax Co., Record of Surveys, p. 154; Circuit Court Archives, Fairfax, Va.

17. Fairfax Co., Deed Book S1:136–40, lease, Pollard to Pritchart; Circuit Court Archives, Fairfax, Va.

18. Beth Mitchell, *Fairfax County Road Orders: 1749–1800* (Charlottesville: Virginia Transportation Research Council, 2003), 135, 144, and 166.

19. Stafford Co., Deed Book S:25 and 37, Philips to Edrington, and 40–43, Hansbrough to Murphy; County Court, Stafford, Va.; LVA Stafford Co. microfilms 1–2. Both tracts adjoined Lewis Pritchett's property.

Hansbrough, but that deed did not survive Stafford County's extensive record losses.[20] Chronology and the tract's acreage indicate it was the land on which the senior Lewis paid taxes in 1782 and 1783.

Lewis "Pritchard," with a household of five "souls" including only one white adult male, paid personal property taxes in Stafford County in 1783. In 1785 Lewis "Pritchet Sr." was taxed, again with just one white adult male in his household. No other Lewis Pritchett paid personal property taxes in Stafford County from 1782 through 1796.[21] Therefore, Lewis "Junr.," owner of a 150-acre tract in 1782–89 and a 240-acre tract from 1790 forward, both in Stafford County, was an absentee landowner.

	Table 1	
	Stafford County Land of Two Pritchett Taxpayers	
YEARS	LEWIS	LEWIS "JUNR."
1782–83	100 acres	150 acres
1784–86	No Lewis Pritchett listings	
1787–89		150 acres
1790–96		240 acres

Source: Virginia Auditor of Public Accounts, Land Tax Books, Stafford County, 1782–1816, entries for Lewis Pritchet (1782, unpaginated), Lewis Prichet (1783, p. 8), Lewis Pritchett Jr. (1782, unpaginated), Lewis Prickett Jr. (1783, p. 8), and Lewis Pritchett Junr. (1787–95, William Mountjoy's District, unpaginated; and 1796, District of George Burroughs, p. 9); manuscript collections, Library of Virginia (LVA), Richmond; LVA land tax microfilm 315.

Apparently only one Lewis Pritchett above age fifteen was taxable in Virginia in 1787.[22] As cited above, Fairfax County tax lists name him from 1782, when the series begins, through 1801. Lewis died in Fairfax County between 22 August 1801, when he served as a witness, and September 1802, when a court ordered the appraisal of his personal estate.[23]

A Stafford County deed dated 1 February 1841, forty years after Lewis died in Fairfax County, shows he owned the 240 acres in Stafford County: Mary A.

---

20. Stafford Co., Deed Book S:331–32, Pritchett to Wood.

21. Virginia Auditor of Public Accounts, Personal Property Tax Books, Stafford County 1782–1813, for Lewis Pritchard (1783, unpaginated) and Lewis Pritchet Sr. (1785, unpaginated); LVA manuscript collections; LVA personal property tax microfilm 327, frames 55 and 79. The 1782 book for Stafford County is missing. Lewis does not appear in 1784 or 1786–96.

22. Schreiner-Yantis and Love, *1787 Census of Virginia*, 3:1063, 1067, and 1860.

23. For the court appearance, see Fairfax Co., Minute Book 1801, p. 163; Circuit Court Archives, Fairfax, Va. For the appraisal order, see Fairfax Co., Will Book I:226; Circuit Court Archives, Fairfax, Va.

Conner of Fairfax County sold her "interest" in a tract with that acreage in Stafford County on the north side of Cannon's Run and adjoining "Hansborough land." Mary received the share "as one of the distributees of Lewis Pritchett dec.ᵈ late of the County of Fairfax."[24]

On 15 October 1776 numerous Stafford County residents, including Lewis Pritchett and Lewis Pritchett "junr.," signed a petition.[25] The younger Lewis apparently moved to Fairfax County between 1776 and 1782.

Supporting Conclusion 3: Lewis's Parentage

A Stafford County adult in 1776, Lewis was born before 1756. Eight years earlier, on 17 February 1748, Lewis Pritchett, son of Lewis and Mary Pritchett, was christened in Stafford County. Baby Lewis's mother, Mary Lattimore, had married Lewis "Pritchet" on 31 March 1744.[26]

The infant, having reached adulthood in 1769, apparently became Lewis Pritchett Jr., Stafford County landowner and 1776 petitioner. He settled in Fairfax County by 1782, where he associated with Philip Pritchett—Fauquier County plaintiff, Fairfax County taxpayer, and eventual Montgomery County, Kentucky, resident. Furthermore, surviving Northern Virginia records suggest no other candidate for Lewis Pritchett christened in 1748.

Supporting Conclusion 4: Philip Not Young Lewis's Son

The close association of Lewis and Philip Pritchett in the Fauquier County trespass suit and Fairfax County suggests they were father and son, but facts disprove it:

- The Fairfax County Lewis Pritchett was christened in 1748, and Philip Pritchett was born in 1762–65. Separated by probably fourteen years—and no more than seventeen—they were too close in age for a likely father and son.
- After Lewis's death in 1801–2 his tax listing was superseded by that of Frances "Pritchert."[27] In 1834 his widow, Frances "Pritchart," lived "now in the state of Ky." and Lewis's Fairfax County land, aside from his widow's dower, was divided among five unnamed heirs.[28] In 1822 they were Sarah

---

24. Stafford Co., Deed Book MM:338, Connor to Heflin; LVA Stafford Co. microfilm 3. Mary, apparently Lewis's granddaughter, also was an heir of Lewis's widow and his unmarried daughter, Sarah. See Fairfax Co., Deed Book D3:462–64, Conner to Allen, 20 January 1838; Circuit Court Archives, Fairfax, Va.

25. Legislative Petitions, Virginia General Assembly, Stafford Co., 1776–1827, petition of 15 October 1776; LVA record group 78, box 238, folder 1, accession 36121; LVA legislative petitions microfilm 187. The same hand, probably that of the younger man, wrote both signatures.

26. George Harrison Sanford King, comp., *The Register of Overwharton Parish; Stafford County Virginia 1723–1758 and Sundry Historical and Genealogical Notes* (Fredericksburg, Va.: privately printed, 1961), 97.

27. Virginia Auditor of Public Accounts, Personal Property Tax List, Fairfax County, 1802, for Frances Pritchert (Robert Moss's district, p. 14).

28. Fairfax Co., Deed Book A2:415–16, Jenkins and Jenkins to Allen.

Pritchett deceased, Elisha Jenkins widower of Susanna Pritchett, Tapley Triar widower of Hetha Pritchett, William Pritchett, and Travis Pritchett.[29]

Lewis and Philip Pritchett may have been closely related, but Lewis's five children are identified and Philip is not among them. The Fairfax County Lewis Pritchett was not Philip's father, but their ages were in range for brothers.

Supporting Conclusion 5: Candidates for Philip's Parents

In Fauquier County on 1 October 1765 John Lattimore's heirs sold "two Negroe slaves named Joe and Solomon." The sellers included "Lewis Pritchard and wife Mary of Stafford Co."[30] Therefore, Lewis Pritchett and Mary Lattimore—whose son Lewis was christened in Stafford County in 1748—lived there in 1765, when Philip Pritchett was born or a young child.

Mary probably was young enough to have had a child born in 1762–65. If she was twenty-one at marriage in 1744, she was thirty-nine in 1762. Even if she was over twenty-one at marriage or Philip was born after 1762, age does not eliminate her as Philip's mother.

Record loss prevents complete reconstruction of the life of Mary's husband, the elder Lewis Pritchett. Surviving sources provide a timeline:

1744	Married Mary Lattimore in Overwharton Parish, Stafford County
1748	Son Lewis christened in Overwharton Parish
1756	Witnessed a Prince William County deed to his father-in-law[31]
1759	Taxed in Fauquier County (the year it was formed from Prince William County)[32]
1765	With wife Mary of Stafford County joined Lattimore heirs in selling slaves in Fauquier County
1776	Signed a legislative petition in Stafford County
1778	Witnessed a Fauquier County deed[33]
1780	Owned land on Aquia Creek waters in Stafford County
1782	Paid tax on one hundred acres in Stafford County
1783	With a five-person household, paid personal property tax and land tax on one hundred acres

---

29. For the division of Lewis's estate and his widow's dower into fifths, see Fairfax Co., Deed Book A3:415–16, Jenkins and Jenkins to Allen; Circuit Court Archives, Fairfax, Va. For his widow's and children's names, see Fairfax Co., Minute Book 1822–23, p. 159, order to sell slaves of Sarah Pritchett, deceased; Circuit Court Archives, Fairfax, Va. Sarah's death as a spinster apparently triggered a late division of her deceased father's property.

30. Fauquier Co., Deed Book 2:508–10, Morless and others to Robertson; County Court, Warrenton, Va.; LVA Fauquier Co. microfilm 1.

31. Prince William Co., Deed Book M:51–55, Young and Smith to Latimore; County Court, Manassas, Va.; LVA Prince William Co. microfilm 3.

32. Joan W. Peters, *The Tax Man Cometh: Land and Property in Colonial Fauquier County, Virginia; Tax Lists from the Fauquier County Court Clerk's Loose Papers; 1759–1782* (Westminster, Md.: Willow Bend, 1999), 3.

33. Fauquier Co., Deed Book 3:527–31, Catlett to Dowdal; LVA Fauquier County microfilm 4.

1785   Paid personal property tax for one male over age twenty-one, two horses, and four cattle

1785   With wife Jane, sold one hundred acres on Aquia Creek, part of the "Savage patent" purchased from Marias Hansbrough via a deed that is now lost

Lewis and Mary stayed much of their lives in Stafford County. They lived in Fauquier County, however, some of the time between 1745 and 1765. The distance was not far—the counties adjoin, and the couple's Stafford County land lay near the county line. Moving to Fauquier County might explain the lack of Overwharton Parish register entries for their family after 1748. Mary died between 1765 and 1785, and Lewis remarried, to Jane, whose surname is unknown. Lewis died perhaps before 7 August 1798, when John Pritchett of Frederick County, Virginia, and "heir of Mary Pritchett who was the daughter of John Latimore," sold 273 acres Lattimore had owned in Fauquier County.[34]

Supporting Conclusion 6: Philip's Next Friend
Philip's close association with Lewis Pritchett in Fairfax County implies Lewis, who settled in Fairfax County by 1782, represented Philip in his 1783 Fauquier County lawsuit. Several points, however, suggest the older Lewis Pritchett, in Stafford County, was Philip's next friend:

- Stafford County adjoins Fauquier County, and Fairfax County does not. Furthermore, defendant Moses Baker's land in Fauquier County lay near Pritchett property in Stafford County. See figure 1.
- Proximity suggests Baker is more likely to have trespassed on Philip and assaulted him in Stafford County than Fairfax County.
- With other Stafford County residents "Phillip Pritchett" signed a petition in 1781.[35] The only known candidate for this petitioner is the 1783 plaintiff. Although he was a minor—age eighteen if born in 1763—he may have wanted to support the petition. The year agrees with Philip's minor status in 1783, first appearance on tax rolls in 1786, and age of forty-five or older in 1810. The petition places Philip in Stafford County in 1781, where the senior Lewis Pritchett headed a household of five "souls" in 1783.
- A minor's next friend was often the minor's parent.[36] Since Fairfax County Lewis Pritchett was not Philip's father, the elder Lewis is the better candidate.
- The senior Lewis Pritchett, living in Stafford County, could easily fill the "next friend" role in nearby Fauquier County. He paid Stafford County taxes in 1782–83 and 1785, and he sold land there in 1785.

34. Fauquier Co., Deed Book 14:269, Pritchett to McRobinson; LVA Fauquier Co. microfilm 7.

35 Legislative Petitions, Virginia General Assembly, Stafford Co., 1776–1827, petition of 14 June and 22 November 1781; LVA record group 78, box 238, folder 13, accession 36121; LVA legislative petitions microfilm reel 187, frame 75.

36. *The Encyclopædia Britannica*, 11th ed. (New York: Encyclopædia Britannica, 1911), s. v. "next friend." The eleventh edition of *The Encyclopædia Britannica* is a "reference of choice" for common-law topics. See Donn Devine, "The Common Law of England," in *NGS Quarterly* 95 (September 2007): 165–78, at 168.

Supporting Conclusion 7: No Other Candidates

Philip Pritchett's close association with Lewis Pritchett in Fairfax County suggests Philip shared Lewis's Stafford County origin. The county's sparse early records yield three sets of candidates for Philip's parents, all married in Overwharton Parish:

1. William Pritchet and Jane Cook, who married 26 January 1742
2. Philip Pritchet and Catherine Cole, who married 24 June 1742
3. Lewis Pritchet and Mary Lattimore, who married 31 March 1744[37]

William Pritchett does not appear in surviving Northern Virginia records after he married Jane Cook. Jane's father bequeathed her two ewes in Fauquier County on 5 January 1760, but her residence is unknown.[38] Philip and Catherine Pritchett had two daughters baptized in Overwharton Parish: Anne, born 4 September 1742; and Catherine, born 28 December 1743.[39] The family apparently moved to Frederick County by 3 June 1746, when "Anne Pritchett aged three Years & Nine months & Catherine Pritchett Aged Two years & six months" were bound to Robert Halfpenny.[40] Philip died there before 3 June 1753, eliminating him as father of a son born in 1762–65.[41]

CONCLUSION

All available evidence indicates Philip Pritchett's parents were Lewis Pritchett and Mary Lattimore, who married in Stafford County, Virginia, in 1744. Philip was born about nineteen years later. He arrived late in his parents' marriage but not too late for them to be plausible parents.

Almost an adult, Philip lived in Stafford County in 1783—one of five members of his father's household—when he sued Moses Baker in adjoining Fauquier County. Because Philip was a minor, his father represented him. Between 1783 and 1786 Philip moved to Fairfax County, joining his older brother Lewis. Philip married probably shortly before 1786, when he began paying taxes.[42] About 1794 he settled in Kentucky.

The identification of Philip Pritchett's parents rests on seven supporting conclusions, each documented and explained. No evidence contradicts the conclusion. The process demonstrates genealogical reasoning—a technique that often can determine kinship.

37. King, comp., *Register of Overwharton Parish*, 97.

38. Fauquier Co., Will Book 1:19, John Cook (1760); County Court, Warrenton, Va.; LVA Fauquier Co. microfilm 31.

39. King, comp., *Register of Overwharton Parish*, 97.

40. Frederick Co., Order Book 2:102; County Court, Winchester, Va.; LVA Frederick Co. microfilm 66.

41. Ibid., 4:161; LVA Frederick Co. microfilm 67. The estate account of "Philip Pritchett deced" was certified in court. The record identifies Philip's administrator as "Philip Pritchett," but no other record of him is known.

42. No Fairfax County or Stafford County civil marriage records from this period survive.

Appendix B
McLain Article

The Three Identities of
Charles D. McLain of Muskegon, Michigan

By Thomas W. Jones, Ph.D., CG, CGL, FASG

Born in 1848–49, married in 1871, and divorced in 1879, Ida's husband should have been found in the thoroughly indexed, every-name 1850, 1860, 1870, and 1880 federal censuses. But he was not. Finding him and his origin required comparing his records with those of another woman's husband and a man with another name.

S ame-name subjects often complicate genealogical research and authors frequently describe techniques for separating their records. Less discussed is the opposite challenge—determining that sources differing in detail or separated by place and time refer to one person. The latter situation can be fortuitous—lineages advance when genealogists show a connection between a person with provable parentage and someone whose parents are unknown.[1]

Records of Charles D. McLain, for example, at first seem to describe three men with different names, birth dates, wives, mothers, occupations, and residences. Family schisms, occupational mobility, and perhaps Charles's desire to hide his past contributed to the discrepancies. Scrutiny of details in the records shows they all pertain to Charles. Combined, they identify his parents.

A LITTLE INFORMATION

Charles's only son to reach adulthood, Earl McLain, probably never saw his father. Earl's mother, however, recounted several facts about the unseen parent:

- Charles D. McLain married Ida May Tucker in Muskegon, Michigan, on 19 August 1871. Fifteen-year-old Ida "rushed" into the marriage because she envied her older sister, who had married a few weeks before.
- Charles and Ida's older children, Percy and Leon, were born in Van Buren County, Michigan, on 26 July 1872 and 30 January 1875, respectively.

© Thomas W. Jones, Ph.D., CG, CGL, FASG; 9232 Arlington Boulevard; Fairfax, VA 22031-2505; Tom@JonesResearchServices.com. Dr. Jones, one of the *NGS Quarterly*'s two lead editors, works as a genealogical researcher, editor, and educator. Like all *NGS Quarterly* articles, his original essay was subjected to blind critiques before its acceptance. To maintain editorial objectivity, Melinde Lutz Sanborn, FASG, edited the piece. The author thanks Susan McGaughey Barillas and Shirley M. De Boer, CG, both of Grand Rapids, Michigan, for research related to this article. All Web sites referenced herein were accessed on 17 January 2008.

1. Thomas W. Jones, "Merging Identities Properly: Jonathan Tucker Demonstrates the Technique," *NGS Quarterly* 88 (June 2000): 111–21.

- Although he was a "good" man, McLain could not support a family.
- A few weeks after Leon's birth during a harsh Michigan winter, Ida's father, Grandpa Tucker, came to visit. He found Ida without firewood, food, or husband. Freezing, she was holding baby Leon, dead apparently from exposure or starvation.
- Grandpa Tucker moved Ida and Percy into his home and arranged for her to divorce McLain.
- After Ida left McLain (apparently after April 1875) she discovered she was pregnant. Earl was born 4 February 1876.[2]

Ida remarried and had five more children.[3] When they were grown Ida and most of her offspring, including Earl McLain and his family, settled in California.[4] One of Earl's daughters became the family's genealogist. Although she documented some of Earl's maternal ancestors, she and a professional researcher could locate only one item concerning Earl's father, the record of his marriage to Ida Tucker.[5] It provides valuable information:

- Charles was native to Michigan—no town or county is specified.
- Twenty-two years old in 1871, he was born in 1848–49.
- Charles lived in the city of Muskegon in 1871.
- His occupation in 1871 was "Sawyer."[6] He likely worked in Michigan's lumber industry cutting felled trees into logs.[7]

These details suggest Charles should appear in the 1870 federal census of Muskegon County, about a year before he married there, and the county's records might identify his parents. However, indexes—except that to his 1871 marriage record—name no Charles McLain (MacLain, McClain, McLaine,

---

2. Bernice (née Leach) (Burlingame) Turner, La Crescenta, Calif., interview by author, 1 November 1980; notes in author's files. The late Mrs. Turner was Ida May (née Tucker) (McLain) Leach's youngest daughter, with whom Ida lived much of her life. Dates are from Ida Leach family Bible record, "loose" family record pages from an unknown Bible; photocopy given author 5 November 1980 by Lennis (née McLain) Harris, now deceased, who received the pages from Mrs. Turner and reported the Bible had been lost or destroyed. Handwriting and ink imply Ida recorded pre-1900 events at one sitting.

3. Ida Leach family Bible record, family pages only.

4. Bernice (née Leach) (Burlingame) Turner, interview by author, 1 November 1980.

5. Ina (née McLain) (Fisher) McPeak to author, letters, 18 June 1972 and 29 June 1973. Mrs. McPeak is deceased.

6. Muskegon Co., Mich., Record of Marriages 2:36, no. 531, McLain-Tucker, 19 August 1871; County Clerk, Muskegon, Mich.; microfilm 1,320,181, Family History Library (FHL), Salt Lake City.

7. William Gerald Rector, "Loggers and Logging to 1870," in *Log Transportation in the Lake States Lumber Industry: 1840–1918* (Glendale, Calif.: Arthur H. Clark, 1953), 72–77, discusses the sawyer's job.

Three Identities of Charles D. McLain of Muskegon, Michigan 103

Figure 1

Southwestern Michigan Counties

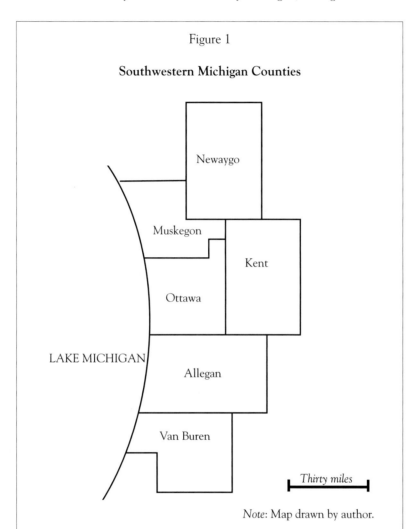

Newaygo

Muskegon

Kent

Ottawa

LAKE MICHIGAN

Allegan

Van Buren

Thirty miles

Note: Map drawn by author.

McLane, McLean, or other variants).[8] Nor is a likely Charles McLain found in earlier censuses.[9]

---

8. Muskegon Co., Chancery Calendar "box 1 folder 1" and vols. 20–25 (1849–1905); Circuit Court, Muskegon, Mich.; FHL microfilms 2,315,513 ("box 1 folder 1" and vols. 20–21), 2,317,627 (vols. 22–24), and 2,317,628 (vol. 25). Muskegon Co., Index to Deeds 3–6 (1838–87); Recorder, Muskegon, Mich.; FHL microfilms 1,377,946 (vol. 3), 1,377,947 (vols. 3–5), and 1,377,948 (vol. 6). Muskegon Co., Index to Marriages: Male (1859–1949); County Clerk, Muskegon, Mich.; FHL microfilm 1,320,181. Muskegon Co., Probate Index (1859–1925); Probate Court Muskegon, Mich.; FHL microfilm 1,392,565, item 3. "Refine Your Search to the 1870 United States Federal Census," *Ancestry.com* (http://www.ancestry.com/search/).

9. *Ancestry.com* (http://www.ancestry.com/search/). Separate searches covered variants of Charles's first name and surname; variables included a range of birth years and birthplaces.

MORE INFORMATION AND FRUITLESS SEARCHES

Tracking Ida's second marriage led to Allegan County, Michigan, two counties south of Muskegon.[10] See figure 1. In summer and fall 1879 an Allegan County court heard Ida's uncontested divorce suit against Charles McLain.[11] Its papers verify descendants' accounts, although his in-laws' affidavits portray Charles more negatively than later family stories. Adding to Charles's identification, his mother-in-law testified he was a carpenter.[12]

On 26 June 1879 officials of Van Buren County, Michigan, the county south of Allegan, subpoenaed Charles at his residence there.[13] This implies Charles would appear in records of Allegan or Van Buren County, if not those of Muskegon or intervening Ottawa County. He is not named in indexes to those county's records, however, except as the defendant in Ida's divorce suit.[14]

The 1880 census should include Charles, probably in one of the above four counties. Strategic searches, however, do not reveal him there or elsewhere.[15] Michigan conducted a state census in 1884, but its Allegan and Van Buren

10. Allegan Co., Mich., Record of Marriages 4:225, no. 892, Leach-McLain, 26 December 1879; County Clerk, Allegan, Mich.; FHL microfilm 1,017,876.

11. Allegan Co., Circuit Court File 1355, Ida M. McLain v. Charles D. McLain, 1879; Circuit Court, Allegan, Mich.; FHL microfilm 2,073,541.

12. Ibid., Mrs. Calista J. Tucker testimony, 22 August 1879. Calista was Ida's mother.

13. Ibid., "Chancery subpoena." Sheriff William Ray certified he had served Charles with the subpoena.

14. For Muskegon Co., see note 8; for the other counties, see the following sources. Allegan Co., Chancery Calendar 2–5 (1867–1900); Waldo Library Archives, Western Michigan University, Kalamazoo; FHL microfilms 1,321,840 (vol. 2), 1,321,841 (vols. 3–4), and 1,321,842 (vols. 4–5). Allegan Co., Index to Deeds 8–15 (1866–1901); Register of Deeds, Allegan, Mich.; FHL microfilms 1,017,879 (vol. 8), 1,017,880 (vols. 9–11), and 1,017,881 (vols. 12–15). Allegan Co., Index to Marriages (1835–1946); County Clerk, Allegan, Mich.; FHL microfilm 1,017,874. Ruth Robbins Monteith, comp., "Wills and Estates: Allegan County, Michigan; 1855–1872," typescript; Michigan State Library, Lansing; FHL microfilm 927,679. Ottawa Co., Mich., Deed Index A–I (1834–1891); Register of Deeds, Grand Haven, Mich.; FHL microfilms 984,267 (vols. A–B), 984,268 (vols. C–E), 984,269 (vols. F–H), and 984,270 (vol. I). Ottawa Co. Index to Marriages (1848–1914); County Clerk, Grand Haven, Mich.; FHL microfilm 984,230. Ottawa Co., General Probate Index (1844–1975); Probate Court, Grand Haven, Mich.; FHL microfilm 984,154. Van Buren Co., Chancery Calendar G (1879–99); Circuit Court, Paw Paw, Mich.; FHL microfilm 2,200,428. Van Buren Co., General Probate Index (1839–1948); Probate Judge, Paw Paw, Mich.; FHL microfilm 1,019,205. Van Buren Co., Grantee-Grantor Index 6–8 (1871–90); Register of Deeds, Paw Paw, Mich.; FHL microfilms 1,019,141 (liber 6) and 1,019,142 (libers 7–8). Van Buren Co., Marriage Index A–B1–B2 and C–D (1836–1905); County Clerk, Paw Paw, Mich.; FHL microfilm 1,019,197.

15. "Refine Your Search to the 1880 United States Federal Census," *Ancestry.com* (http://www .ancestry.com/search/). Separate searches included variants of Charles's given name, surname, age, occupation, and Michigan birthplace.

Table 1
Charles D. McLain Data from Four Newaygo County Censuses

YEAR	AGE	BIRTH DATE	OCCUPATION	BIRTHPLACE	PARENTS' BIRTHPLACES
1894	40	1853–54	Teamster	Michigan	Michigan, Michigan[a]
1900	46	January 1854	House Carpenter	Michigan	Ohio, Ohio[b]
1910	54	1855–56	Carpenter	Michigan	Michigan, Michigan[c]
1920	58	1861–62	Carpenter	Michigan	Vermont, Canada[d]

Note: The 1910 and 1920 enumerations report that Charles worked in the "House" industry. The birthplaces specified for his parents in 1920 seem confused with those of Emma's parents: Canada for both in 1894 and 1900, Canada and Vermont in 1910, Michigan and Vermont in 1920, and Canada for both in 1930. For the latter, see 1930 U.S. census, Newaygo Co., Mich., population schedule, Brooks Twp., Village of Newaygo, Enumeration District (ED) 62-7, sheet 2B, dwelling/family 45, Emma McLain; National Archives and Records Administration (NARA) microfilm publication T626, roll 1,015. Except for 1900, birth dates are calculated from ages reported in the census.

   a.   1894 Michigan census, Newaygo Co., Brooks Twp., page 32, dwell. 156, fam. 158; Record Group 79-98, Library of Michigan; unnumbered microfilm, Grand Rapids Public Library, Grand Rapids, Mich.

   b.   1900 U.S. census, Newaygo Co., Mich., pop. sch., Brooks Twp., ED 89, sheet 4, dwell. 72, fam. 77; NARA microfilm T623, roll 735. This enumeration records each person's month and year of birth reported by an unidentified informant.

   c.   1910 U.S. census, Newaygo Co., Mich., pop. sch., Brooks Twp., Newaygo Village, ED 115, sheet 7A, dwell. 112, fam. 116; NARA microfilm T624, roll 666.

   d.   1920 U.S. census, Newaygo Co., Mich., pop. sch., Brooks Twp., Newaygo Village, ED 129, sheet 5B, dwell. 156, fam. 159; NARA microfilm T625, roll 787.

County schedules are missing.[16] No Charles McLain appears in its Muskegon and Ottawa County indexes.[17]

Born in 1848–49, married in 1871, and divorced in 1879, Charles should appear in the thoroughly indexed, every-name 1850, 1860, 1870, and 1880 federal censuses. He does not. He seemingly materialized out of nowhere in 1871 to wed Ida and disappeared after a few unhappy years of marriage. Ida's descendants speculated he had died, changed his name, or moved to Canada. Finding him and his origin required comparing his records with those of another woman's husband and a man with another name.

ANOTHER WOMAN'S HUSBAND

A census taken more than twenty years after the McLains' 1879 divorce seems to identify the elusive ex-husband. In 1900 "Chas D McLain," a "house carpenter" born in Michigan, lived in Michigan's Newaygo County (adjoining

16. LeRoy Barnett, "State Censuses of Michigan—A Tragedy of Lost Treasures," *Family Trails* 6 (Summer–Fall 1978): 1–29. See especially "Existing State Censuses of Michigan," pp. 21–23.

17. "1884 Census," *Muskegon County Genealogical Society* (http://www.rootsweb.com/~mimcgs/ 1884census.html). For Ottawa County, see "West Michigan Census: Search," *Western Michigan Genealogical Society* (http://data.wmgs.org/MichiganCensus/FMPro?-db=MichiganCensus&-lay= Listing&-format=search.htm&-view).

Muskegon County to the northeast) with wife Emma and four daughters born 1887–99.[18] His name, birthplace, and occupation match those of Ida's Charles D. McLain. Also compatible are the location of Charles's household and its lack of children born during the McLain-Tucker marriage years. His January 1854 birth date, however, is too late for the twenty-two-year-old man Ida married in 1871. Other censuses suggest Emma's husband was born even later—see table 1. Moreover, Charles's 1910 enumeration identifies the marriage to Emma as his first.[19] Regardless, the parallels between Ida's husband and the Newaygo County Charles McLain are compelling. Information from reliable sources was needed to clarify Charles's identity.

Unlike Ida's Charles, Emma's Charles McLain left several records. Their daughter identified her parents as Emma Cope and "Chas." McLain.[20] As Emma E. Cope and "D." McLain, they married in Kent County, Michigan, on 21 October 1886. Giving his age as thirty-two (implying birth in 1853–54), the record says this bridegroom worked in the "Lumber Business" and resided in South Haven, Michigan, in Van Buren County.[21] Emma's husband's name, occupation, and location, and his marriage's date are compatible with the 1879 divorcé, but his age is not. His obituary, however, reports his birth on 13 January 1849, matching the age of Ida Tucker's first husband.[22] The 1 February 1849 birthday calculated from his death record also matches.[23]

A will or estate record might name his children, but no such McLain record in Newaygo County—where Charles lived for almost forty years, owned property, and died—exists.[24] His obituary identifies as offspring only his daughters with

18. 1900 U.S. census, Newaygo Co., Mich., population schedule, Brooks Twp., Enumeration District (ED) 89, sheet 4, dwelling 72, family 77, Chas[.] D[.] McLain household; National Archives and Records Administration (NARA) microfilm publication T623, roll 735.

19. 1910 U.S. census, Newaygo Co., Mich., pop. sch., Brooks Twp., Newaygo Village, ED 115, sheet 7A, dwell. 112, fam. 116, Charles D. McLain; NARA microfilm T624, roll 666.

20. Newaygo Co., Mich., Marriage Record 4:232, no. 435, Peterson-McLain, 3 October 1908; County Clerk, White Cloud, Mich.; FHL microfilm 1,006,427.

21. Kent Co., Mich., Marriage Record 8:213, no. 15,493, McLain-Cope, 21 October 1886; County Clerk, Grand Rapids, Mich.

22. "[Charles D. McLain] Obituary," *Newaygo Republican*, Newaygo, Mich., 30 April 1925, page 1, col. 1.

23. Newaygo Co., Death Record 3:66, Charles McLain, 21 April 1925; County Clerk, White Cloud, Mich.; FHL microfilm 1,006,425. The record gives McLain's age as seventy-six years, two months, and twenty days. The informant, not named, probably was Charles's widow or one of his daughters, all adults at the time.

24. Shirley M. De Boer, Grand Rapids, Mich., to author, letter, 14 December 2007. Ms. De Boer, a professional researcher holding the Certified Genealogist credential, reports "using various spellings, the probate court of Newaygo had no listing for Charles Mc Lain." His widow's obituary reports "the couple built the home on Schoolhouse hill where Mrs. McLain resided until her death," so Charles's heirs did not dispose of the property until after 1948. See "Rites Held on Sunday for Mrs. Emma McLain, Long-time Local Resident," *Newaygo Republican*, Newaygo, Mich., 18 March 1948, page 1, col. 4.

Emma.[25] Eight points, however, suggest that Earl McLain was Charles's son—that after Earl's mother divorced Charles he married Emma Cope:

- The two husbands' names, including middle initial, are identical.
- Both worked as carpenters and in the lumber industry.
- Chronology fits—the McLain-Cope marriage followed the McLain divorce by seven years.
- The last record of Ida's spouse places him in Van Buren County, Michigan. The first record of Emma's husband says he resided there.
- Ida's husband was born in Michigan in 1848–49. Emma's spouse reportedly was born in Michigan on 13 January or 1 February 1849. (Inconsistent censuses reporting Charles's birth between 1854 and 1862 may be discounted. Wishing to appear closer in age to Emma, born in 1865, Charles may have trimmed five years from his age when they married.)[26]
- Charles's reported age when he married Emma—thirty-two years—is late for a first marriage.
- Charles may not have told Emma of his previous marriage and divorce, causing him or others to claim his union with Emma was his first.
- If two Charles D. McLains of comparable age lived simultaneously in southwestern Michigan, they appear concurrently in no known listing.

This conclusion may explain what became of Charles after Ida divorced him, but it does not reveal his origin. Also, information about his parents might strengthen the argument or disprove it.

A MAN WITH ANOTHER NAME

Michigan marriage records did not name the parties' parents when Charles D. McLain married Ida and when D. McLain married Emma. Two undocumented online databases, however, may identify McLain's mother and father. They offer conflicting information on the man who married Emma Cope in Kent County on 21 October 1886:

1. Charles D. "Mc Lain," born 13 January 1849 in Grand Haven, Ottawa County, Michigan, parents unnamed[27]
2. David R. McLain, born about 1854 in Sparta, Kent County, Michigan, son of James McLain and Phebe Wright[28]

Referring to the same husband, both entries cannot be entirely accurate. If correct regarding the marriage, however, they reveal the parents of Charles D. McLain who settled in Newaygo County.

---

25. "[Charles D. McLain] Obituary," *Newaygo Republican*, Newaygo, Mich., 30 April 1925, page 1, col. 1.

26. Kent Co., Mich., Marriage Record 8:213, no. 15,493, McLain-Cope, 21 October 1886.

27. Robert Allen DeVowe, comp., "Ancestry World Tree Project: Newaygo County," *Ancestry .com* (http://awt.ancestry.com).

28. DeWayne G. Baker, comp., "Ancestry World Tree Project: Baker Odyssey," *Ancestry.com* (http://awt.ancestry.com).

The first entry seems drawn from *FamilySearch*'s Ancestral File database.[29] The family's names, dates, and other details match those of the Newaygo County household of Charles and Emma McLain in 1894, 1900, 1910, 1920, and 1930.[30] Charles's death record reports his birth in Grand Haven, in Ottawa County, Michigan, on 1 February 1849 to James McLain and Mary Mapes.[31]

Those parents cannot be confirmed in a birth or census record. Michigan did not document births before 1867.[32] Moreover, Ottawa and surrounding counties have no marriage record for James McLain or a McLain groom to a Mapes bride before 1870.[33] Indexes to the 1850, 1860, 1870, and 1880 Michigan censuses neither lead to Charles McLain born about 1849 with an apparent parent James or Mary nor reveal James McLain with apparent wife Mary.[34]

Like the second online database entry, the record of "D." McLain's marriage to Emma says he was born in Kent County, just east of Ottawa County. A Kent County resident's Civil War pension file, correlated with other original records, seems to corroborate Emma's husband's parents as Phebe and James McLain:[35]

---

29. Alvin L. Monroe, submitter, Charles D. "Mc Lain" family group record, AF93-104233, *FamilySearch* (http://www.familysearch.org).

30. 1894 Michigan census, Newaygo Co., pop. sch., Brooks Twp., p 32, dwell. 156, fam. 158, Charles D. McLane household; Record Group (RG) 79-98, Library of Michigan, Lansing; unnumbered microfilm, Grand Rapids Public Library, Grand Rapids, Mich. Also, 1900 U.S. census, Newaygo Co., Mich., pop. sch., Brooks Twp., ED 89, sheet 4, dwell. 72, fam. 77, Chas[.] D[.] McLain household. Also, 1910 U.S. census, Newaygo Co., Mich., pop. sch., Brooks Twp., Newaygo Village, ED 115, sheet 7A, dwell. 112, fam. 116, Charles D. McLain household. Also, 1920 U.S. census, Newaygo Co., Mich., pop. sch., Brooks Twp., Newaygo Village, ED 129, sheet 5B, dwell. 156, fam. 159, Charles D. McLain household; NARA microfilm T625, roll 787. Also, 1930 U.S. census, Newaygo Co., Mich., pop. sch., Brooks Twp., Village of Newaygo, ED 62-7, sheet 2b, dwell./fam. 45, Emma McLain; NARA microfilm T626, roll 1015.

31. Newaygo Co., Death Record 3:66, Charles McLain, 21 April 1925.

32. "Circular No. 19—State and Local Vital Records," *Archives of Michigan* (http://www .michigan.gov/documents/mhc_sa_circular19_49707_7.pdf).

33. Allegan Co., Index to Marriages (1835–1946); Muskegon Co., Index to Marriages: Male (1859–1949); and Ottawa Co., Index to Marriages (1848–1914). Also, Sophie de Marsac Campau Chapter, D.A.R. (Grand Rapids, Mich.), "Marriages Prior to 1870 in Kent County, Michigan," typescript (1937); National Society Daughters of the American Revolution Library, Washington, D.C.; FHL microfilm 857,307. Also, "Early Marriages: Newaygo County; The Dibean Collection," *RootsWeb* (http://www.rootsweb.com/~minewayg/dibean.html).

34. *Ancestry.com* (http://www.ancestry.com/search/). Separate searches covered variants of Charles, James, and Mary's surname; variables included a range of birth years and Michigan and Ohio birthplaces.

35. James McLain (Pvt., Co. D, 2 Mich. Cav., Civil War) pension no. S.C. 222,625, Case Files of Approved Pension Applications . . . 1861–1934; Civil War and Later Pension Files; Department of Veterans Affairs, RG 15; National Archives (NA), Washington, D.C.

Three Identities of Charles D. McLain of Muskegon, Michigan   109

July 1827	James McLain was born in Knox County, Ohio.[36] His parents were David and Mary (née Severe) McLain.[37]
15 March 1845	James married Phebe Wright in Knox County.[38]
15 September 1845	Phebe left James.[39]
about 8 January 1846	Their daughter Sarah McLain was born in Knox County.[40]
8 August 1846	Claiming desertion and adultery, James filed for divorce.[41]
10 June 1847	After two continuances, the Knox County Court of Common Pleas dismissed the McLains' divorce suit.[42]
1849–52	Reconciled, James and Phebe had a son, David R., born in Michigan.[43]
1851–52	James moved to Michigan, presumably from Ohio.[44]
1852–53	Their apparent daughter Catherine was born in Michigan.[45]

36. For the date, see Mary McLain affidavit, 19 September 1885, Stewart J. McLain (Pvt., Co. E, 21 Mich. Inf., Civil War) pension no. W.C. 222,094, Case Files of Approved Pension Applications . . . 1861–1934; Civil War and Later Pension Files; Department of Veterans Affairs, RG 15, NA–Washington. Stewart J. McLain was James's brother; Mary was their mother. For James's birthplace, see James McLain discharge certificate, in James McLain pension no. S.C. 222,625, RG 15, NA.

37. William H. Simons, affidavit, 14 October 1885, and Mary McLain, affidavit, 19 September 1885, Stewart J. McLain pension no. W.C. 222,094, RG 15, NA. For Mary's maiden name, see Knox Co., Ohio, Marriage Record 1808–38, p. 125, McClain-Severe, 22 December 1825; Probate Court, Mount Vernon, Ohio; FHL microfilm 1,294,304.

38. Knox Co., Ohio, Marriage Certificates (chronologically arranged), "Mclane"-Wright, 15 March 1845; Probate Court, Mount Vernon, Ohio; FHL microfilm 2,243,649, frame 4,545.

39. Knox Co., Common Pleas case file 995, box 11, McLain v. McLain, James McLain petition; Probate Court, Mount Vernon, Ohio; FHL microfilm 2,240,090, frames 2,476–81.

40. On 8 August 1846 James said he and Phebe had a daughter "about seven months old." See Knox Co., Common Pleas case file 995, box 11, McLain v. McLain, James McLain petition. James's 1860 household included a child Sarah, age fourteen years. See 1860 U.S. census, Kent Co., Mich., pop. sch., Paris Twp., Grand Rapids post office, p. 66, dwell. 566, fam. 477, Sarah McLane; NARA microfilm M653, roll 550.

41. Knox Co., Common Pleas case file 995, box 11, McLain v. McLain. The file contains only James's petition and a subpoena for Phebe's appearance to answer it.

42. Knox Co., Minutes O:74, 229, and 361, McLain v. McLain; Court of Common Pleas, Mount Vernon, Ohio; FHL microfilm 1,294,314.

43. 1860 U.S. census, Kent Co., Mich., pop. sch., Paris Twp., Grand Rapids post office, p. 66, dwell. 566, fam. 477, J. McLane, Phebe McLane, and David McLane. 1870 U.S. census, Muskegon Co., Mich., pop. sch., Muskegon, Ward 3, p. 30, dwell. 204, fam. 201, Phebe McLane and Daniel [David] McLane; NARA microfilm M593, roll 692. For James's relationship to his son and his son's middle initial, see Kent Co., probate file 4735, James McLain will; Probate Court, Grand Rapids, Mich.

44. 1884 Michigan census, Kent Co., Sparta Twp., p. 31, fam. 167, James McLain; RG 80-75, Library of Michigan; unnumbered microfilm, Grand Rapids Public Library. The schedule says James was born in Ohio and had lived in Michigan for thirty-two years.

45. 1860 U.S. census, Kent Co., Mich., pop. sch., Paris Twp., Grand Rapids post office, p. 66, dwell. 566, fam. 477, Catherine McLane.

110   *National Genealogical Society Quarterly*

20–21 October 1853	Orilla McLain married Jesse Mapes at James and Phebe McLain's house in Alpine Township, Kent County, Michigan.[46]
1855–61	James "was farming summers and lumbering winters in Kent Co.[,] Mich."[47]
1 June 1860	"J. McLane," a thirty-year-old farm laborer, lived in Paris Township, Kent County. His household included Phebe McLane, age thirty, and children Sarah, fourteen; David, eight; and Catherine, seven. The census reports Michigan birthplaces, apparently erroneous in some cases, for everyone in the household.[48]
14 November 1861	James McLain, thirty-four years old, enlisted at Paris in Company D, 2nd Michigan Cavalry.[49]
about 1862	Phebe and James McLain "seperated."[50]
14 August 1865	Discharged in Indianapolis from military duty, McLain went to Lansing, Michigan, for "a short stay" and settled in Kent County's Alpine Township.[51]
1 June 1870	Forty-four-year-old Ohio-born James "McLane," a farm laborer, was enumerated about twenty-five miles north of Alpine in the village of Newaygo—see figure 2. Harriet E. McLane, a thirty-six-year-old housekeeper born in Michigan, lived with him.[52] Depositions by McLain and later by his widow do not mention Harriet.[53] James was still married to Phebe, who lived in Muskegon, about thirty miles southwest of

---

46. Malissa McLain, affidavit, 20 November 1885, and James McLain and Malissa A. Chase, affidavit, 22 February 1884, Jesse Mapes (Pvt., Co. E, 3 Mich. Inf., Civil War) pension no. S.C. 141,891, Case Files of Approved Pension Applications . . . 1861–1934; Civil War and Later Pension Files; Department of Veterans Affairs, RG 15, NA. Mapes married James and Malissa McLain's sister. The witnesses differ in the date they report for the wedding, for which no civil record exists. See Sophie de Marsac Campau Chapter, D.A.R., "Marriages Prior to 1870 in Kent County, Michigan."

47. James McLain, statement, 11 April 1881, James McLain pension no. S.C. 222,625, RG 15, NA.

48. 1860 U.S. census, Kent Co., Mich., pop. sch., Paris Twp., Grand Rapids post office, p. 66, dwell. 566, fam. 477, J. McLane household. The enumerator visited on 25 June 1860.

49. James McLain, statement, 11 April 1881, James McLain pension no. S.C. 222,625, RG 15, NA.

50. Simeon R. Wright, affidavit, 16 December 1889, James McLain pension no. S.C. 222,625, RG 15, NA. Wright identified McLain's ex-wife, Phebe, as his sister.

51. James McLain, statement, 11 April 1881, James McLain pension no. S.C. 222,625, RG 15, NA.

52. 1870 U.S. census, Newaygo Co., Mich., pop. sch., Village of Newaygo, p. 18, dwell./fam. 147, James McLane household; NARA microfilm M593, roll 693. The enumerator visited the household on 12 July 1870.

53. James McLain, statements, 9 and 11 April 1881, Margeanna McLain, "Widow's Declaration for Pension," 21 May 1889, Margeanna McLain affidavit, 10 July 1889, and "Margie anna" McLain, "Application for Widow's Pension," 31 March 1891, James McLain pension no. S.C. 222,625, RG 15, NA.

Three Identities of Charles D. McLain of Muskegon, Michigan   111

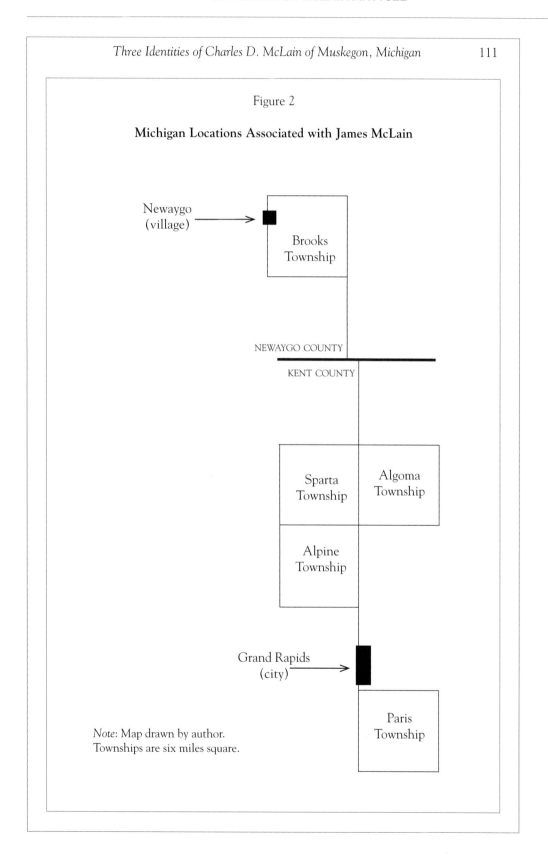

Figure 2

Michigan Locations Associated with James McLain

Newaygo (village)

Brooks Township

NEWAYGO COUNTY

KENT COUNTY

Sparta Township

Algoma Township

Alpine Township

Grand Rapids (city)

Paris Township

Note: Map drawn by author.
Townships are six miles square.

112 *National Genealogical Society Quarterly*

Figure 3

Image from 1870 Census

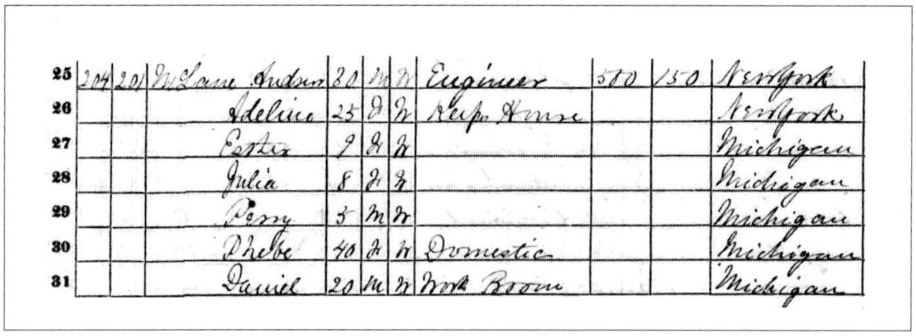

25	204	201	McLane Andrew	30	M	W	Engineer	500	150	New York
26			Adeline	25	F	W	Keep. House			New York
27			Ester	9	F	W				Michigan
28			Julia	8	F	W				Michigan
29			Perry	3	M	W				Michigan
30			Phebe	40	F	W	Domestic			Michigan
31			Daniel	20	M	W	Work Room			Michigan

Source: 1870 U.S. census, Muskegon Co., Mich., population schedule, Muskegon, Ward 3, p. 30, dwelling 204, family 201, Andrew McLane household; National Archives and Records Administration microfilm publication M593, roll 692.

Newaygo, with their son, David, listed as "Daniel McLane."[54] (When written carelessly, *Daniel* can be indistinguishable from *David*. The census entry does appear to say *Daniel*—see figure 3—perhaps because the enumerator misread *David* when he copied the pages as the law required.)[55]

19 May 1874 — The Newaygo County Circuit Court granted Phebe McLain a divorce from James on grounds of "several acts of adultery."[56]

7 September 1874 — James, a forty-seven-year-old Ohio native, married Mrs. Margianna (née Davis) Greenman in Englishville, a village

54. 1870 U.S. census, Muskegon Co., Mich., pop. sch., Muskegon, Ward 3, p. 30, dwell. 204, fam. 201, Phebe McLane and Daniel [David] McLane. The visitation date was 26 July 1870. Phebe and "Daniel" appear to have been boarding in the Andrew McLane household. Andrew's relationship to James McLain, if any, is unknown.

55. The Census Act of 1850 governed the 1870 census. See "The Ninth Census: 1870," in U.S. Department of Commerce, *Measuring America: The Decennial Censuses from 1790 to 2000* (Washington, D.C.: U.S. Census Bureau, 2002), 131. For the 1850 act, see United States Congress, *U.S. Statutes at Large*, vol. 9 (Boston: Little, Brown, 1862), "Chap. XI—An Act providing for the taking of the seventh and subsequent censuses of the United States . . . ," 428–36, especially section 11 (p. 430), which instructs each assistant marshal to make two copies of his original returns, file the original with the respective county clerk, and submit the two copies to the marshal. Section 5 (p. 429), requires the marshal to transmit one copy to the secretary of his state or territory and the other to the U.S. Secretary of the Interior. If these regulations were followed, the 1870 census microfilmed at the National Archives consists of handwritten copies, not original schedules.

56. James McLain pension no. S.C. 222,625, RG 15, NA, contains a copy of the divorce decree certified by the Newaygo Co. clerk. A professional researcher could not locate the suit's papers in Newaygo County, Western Michigan University, or the Michigan State Archives, suggesting they were destroyed. See De Boer to author, letter, 14 December 2007.

Three Identities of Charles D. McLain of Muskegon, Michigan 113

	in Alpine Township. David McLain of Alpine (apparently James's father, brother, or son) witnessed the marriage.[57]
1879	McLain's "family was broke up," and he moved one township north, from Alpine to Sparta.[58]
15 June 1880	Fifty-three-year-old James, a laborer, lived with his widowed mother, Mary McLain, in Sparta.[59] His wife, "Maggie" McLain, lived in Grand Rapids, the Kent County seat, with her three Greenman children.[60]
15 April 1884	McLain was admitted to The National Home for Disabled Volunteer Soldiers, Central Branch, near Dayton, Ohio.[61]
June 1884	James, an Ohio native, age fifty-six, reportedly a "Widower," and apparently on furlough from the soldiers' home, was enumerated with his mother in Sparta.[62]
2 January 1885	McLain was discharged from the soldiers home.[63]
1 April 1885	With money from his son, David R. McLain, James purchased forty acres in Algoma Township (east of Sparta).[64]
10 December 1885	"Of the Township of Algoma," McLain wrote his will. He directed that his estate "be equally divided share and share alike between my mother and my Brother David C. McLain and my sisters Orilla M. Mapes and Malissa A. McLain and also my son David R. McLain on condition that he comes back to stay at my present place of residence within one year from this present time."[65]

---

57. Mich. Secretary of State, "Return of Marriages in the County of Kent," 1874, 2:151, no. 4374, McLain-Greenman, 7 September 1874; Mich. Department of Health, Lansing; FHL microfilm 2,342,457. Margianna applied twice for a Civil War pension as James's widow. See Margeanna McLain, "Widow's Declaration for Pension," 21 May 1889, and "Margie anna" McLain, "Application for Widow's Pension," 31 March 1891, James McLain pension no. S.C. 222,625, RG 15, NA. The file includes a certified transcription of the county-level marriage record, referencing Kent Co., Marriages 4:145.

58. James McLain, affidavit, 9 April 1881, James McLain pension no. S.C. 222,625, RG 15, NA.

59. 1880 U.S. census, Kent Co., Mich., pop. sch., Sparta Village, ED 114, p. 26, dwell./fam. 289; NARA microfilm T9, roll 587, Mary McLain and James McClain.

60. 1880 U.S. census, Kent Co., Mich., pop. sch., Grand Rapids, ED 149, p. 24, 153 Third Street, dwell. 229, fam. 262, Maggie McLain household; NARA microfilm T9, roll 588.

61. "Notice of Admission of James McLain," 17 April 1884, James McLain pension no. S.C. 222,625, RG 15, NA.

62. 1884 Michigan census, Kent Co., Sparta, p. 31, fam. 167, James McLain and Mary McLain.

63. "Notice of Discharge of James McLain," 2 January 1885, James McLain pension no. S.C. 222,625, RG 15, NA.

64. Kent Co., Deeds 170:397, Barber to McLain; Recorder, Grand Rapids, Mich.; FHL microfilm 1,392,950. For the money's source, see Kent Co., Mich., probate file 4735, David R. McLain claim, 14 December 1886.

65. Kent Co., Probate file 4735, James McLain will.

14 December 1885   James McLain died at Algoma Township.[66]

18 January 1886   James's executor—his brother David C. McLain—identified James's heirs as his sister Orilla M. Mapes of Sparta, sister Melissa O. McLain of Sparta, son David R. McLain of Newaygo, mother Mary McLain of Sparta, and brother David C. McLain of Algoma.[67]

18 August 1899   James's mother, Mary McLain, died.[68] Because she outlived James, her heirs should include his offspring. Mary, however, left no will or other estate record.[69]

When compared with information about Charles D. McLain who married Emma Cope, details related to the above chronology suggest he was James's son, David R. McLain:

- An unknown informant for Charles's death record—probably his widow or daughter—identified Charles's father as James McLain. The man whose life is detailed above apparently was the only James McLain enumerated in southwestern Michigan of the right age to be Charles's father. His only son appearing in 1860 was David McLain.

- When he married Emma, Charles was recorded as "D. McLain," implying his name began with *D*, like David.

- Charles D. McLain reportedly was born in Kent County and as late as 1 February 1854. James and Phebe McLain settled in Kent County before 21 October 1853.

- Reported posthumously, Charles's birth in Ottawa County around 1850 connects him to James McLain. James's paternal grandparents, brother, three uncles, and several cousins lived in Ottawa County in 1850.[70] (James's parents and siblings, however, still lived in Ohio in 1850;[71] James's 1850 household has

---

66. Kent Co., Probate file 4735, "Petition for Appointment of Administrator," 18 January 1886. James's estranged widow reported he died on "Dec 16ᵗʰ 1885" and "on or about the 7 day of Dec., 1885." See (for 7 December) "Margeanna" McLain, "Widow's Declaration for Pension," 21 May 1889, and (for 16 December) "Margie anna" McLain, "Declaration for Widow's Pension," 31 March 1891, James McLain pension no. S.C. 222,625, RG 15, NA. James's death does not appear in indexes to Kent County death records for 1885. For the county-level search, see DeBoer to author, letter, 14 December 2007. For state level, see Mich. Secretary of State, "Return of Deaths in the County of Kent," 1885; FHL microfilm 2,363,630.

67. Kent Co., probate file 4735, "Petition for Appointment of Administration."

68. Pension Agent, Detroit, Mich., to Commissioner of Pensions, Washington, D.C., "Pensioner Dropped," Stewart J. McLain pension no. W.C. 222,094, RG 15, NA.

69. Susan McGaughey Barillas, Grand Rapids, Mich., to author, e-mail, 14 February 2008.

70. 1850 U.S. census, Ottawa Co., Mich., pop. sch., Chester Twp., p. 21, dwells./fams. 223–24 and 228–29; NARA microfilm M432, roll 361, John J. McLain, Aaron J. McLain, Aaron McLain Jr., and Aaron McLain households. Two documented compilations show McLain relationships: DeWayne G. Baker, *Baker/McClain Odyssey: 1774–2000* (Lapeer, Mich.: privately printed, 2000); and Denise Crawford, "Descendants of Aaron McClain and Elizabeth\Anna (—)," *Pedigree Resource File*, CD-ROM 18 (Salt Lake City: Church of Jesus Christ of Latter-day Saints, 2000).

71. 1850 U.S. census, Knox Co., Ohio, pop. sch., Milford Twp., p. 95, dwell. 1324, fam. 1336, David McLain household; NARA microfilm M432, roll 700.

Table 2

David McLain's Tools

One vice and Screw	One wood chisel
nine planes	Three cold chisels
Two gauges	Nine old files
Two mallets	One Saw Swedge [swage]
One reveting hammer	two monkey wrenches
One brace	two Spoke Shaves
nine bits	4 awls
One Square	Two fair compasses
two try Squares	three hand Saws
One Oil Stone	One Compass Saw
One bevel Square	

Source: Kent Co., Ohio, Circuit Court File 14,209, "Appeal File, 19 March 1887, In the Matter of the Estate of James McLain, Deceased vs. Appeal of David C. McLain from Probate Court," packet containing "Levy on personal property," 5 December 1887, and return of sale by sheriff, 17 December 1887; Circuit Court, Grand Rapids, Mich. Capitalization and spelling follow those in the earlier document. Listed with the tools is "One Tool Chest."

For descriptions, illustrations, and uses of these tools, see Henry C. Mercer, *Ancient Carpenters' Tools: Illustrated and Explained, Together with the Implements of the Lumberman, Joiner, and Cabinet Maker in Use in the Eighteenth Century* (Doylestown, Pa.: The Bucks County Historical Society, 1960). Despite its subtitle, the book provides detailed information on nineteenth-century carpentry tools.

not been found in Michigan or Ohio.) Perhaps after moving to Michigan, James and Phebe lived temporarily with his Ottawa County relatives before settling in Kent County. Their son may have been born during a brief stay in Ottawa County. Having grown up in Kent County, he may have implied it was his birthplace when he married Emma there, or the recorder may have assumed it.

- Whether Charles was born in Kent or Ottawa County, both are likely residences for James and Phebe when their son, David, was born.
- For $250 David R. McLain quitclaimed his interest in his late father's land.[72] He claimed from James's estate, however, $330 he had given James to buy the land plus $36.80 interest. Disallowing reimbursement because of the quitclaim, the judge required David to pay the court costs of disputing his claim.[73] David didn't pay, and his uncle David C. McLain sued him. Absent the payment, the court ordered the sheriff to seize and sell David's personal

72. Kent Co., Deeds 171:265–66, David R. McLain to Elizabeth L. McLain, two quitclaims dated 5 June 1886. Elizabeth L. McLain was married to David C. McLain, David's uncle. See Kent Co., Marriage Register 4:260, McClain-Miller, 26 July 1865.

73. Kent Co., probate file 4735, Robert M. Montgomery ruling, 1 June 1887.

property, a chest containing carpenter's tools.[74] See table 2. David R. McLain, therefore, was a carpenter, as was Emma's Charles D. McLain.

- David McLain was "single" on 15 June 1886 when he quitclaimed his share of his father's land.[75] Charles D. McLain, who married Emma on 21 October 1886, probably was single the preceding June.

- David (or "Daniel") McLain appears in the 1860 and 1870 censuses; a likely Charles McLain does not.

- Judging from the specificity of the residences of James's other heirs, David R. McLain lived in Newaygo village in January 1886, not elsewhere in Newaygo County. Charles D. McLain was "employed" in that community before 21 October 1886, when he married Emma, "a life-long resident of Newaygo."[76]

- D. McLain married Emma in Kent County's Sparta Township, where James McLain lived in 1880 and 1884.

- The 1900 census says Charles's parents were born in Ohio, the only credible out-of-state birthplaces his enumerations give them—see table 1. James was born in Ohio, where he and Phebe married, and where Phebe probably was born.[77]

- The posthumous identification of Charles D. McLain's mother as Mary Mapes is unsubstantiated. The informant, probably Charles's widow or daughter, may have confused his relatives—especially likely if he was alienated from his family. David R. McLain's *grand*mother was Mary. Because she died thirteen years after Charles married Emma, the unnamed informant for Charles's death certificate may have known or heard of her. David's Mapes kin were children and grandchildren of his aunt Orilla Mapes.

---

74. Kent Co., Circuit Court file 14,209, "Appeal File, 19 March 1887, In the Matter of the Estate of James McLain, Deceased vs. Appeal of David C. McLain from Probate Court," packet containing "Levy on personal property," 5 December 1887, and return of sale by sheriff, 17 December 1887; Circuit Court, Grand Rapids, Mich.

75. Kent Co., Deeds 171:265–66, David R. McLain to Elizabeth L. McLain, two quitclaims dated 5 June 1886.

76. "Rites Held on Sunday for Mrs. Emma McLain, Long-time Local Resident," *Newaygo Republican*, Newaygo, Mich., 18 March 1948, page 1, col. 4, mentions McLain's employment in Newaygo before he married Emma. The informant may have been one of their daughters.

77. Phebe's younger brother reportedly was born in Ohio in 1830–31 to Pennsylvania-born parents. See 1880 U.S. census, Kent Co., Mich., pop. sch., Plainfield Twp., ED 120, p. 27, dwell. 241, fam. 242, Simeon R. Wright. Simeon also reportedly was born in Canada. See Wm. M. Smith, "Surgeon's Certificate" (16 December 1908), Simeon R. Wright (Pvt., Co. G, 17 Mich. Inf., Civil War) pension no. S.C. 109,632, Case Files of Approved Pension Applications . . . 1861–1934; Civil War and Later Pension Files; Department of Veterans Affairs, RG 15, NA. In any case, the siblings' unnamed father lived in Hilliar Township, Knox County, Ohio, in 1846. See Knox Co., Common Pleas case file 995, box 11, McLain v. McLain, James McLain petition. The only known sources showing Phebe's birthplace, however, say she was born in Michigan in 1829–30. See 1860 U.S. census, Kent Co., Mich., pop. sch., Paris Twp., Grand Rapids post office, p. 66, dwell. 566, fam. 477, Phebe McLain; and 1870 U.S. census, Muskegon Co., Mich., pop. sch., Muskegon, Ward 3, p. 30, dwell. 204, fam. 201, Phebe McLane.

Three Identities of Charles D. McLain of Muskegon, Michigan   117

Details related to James McLain also support the probability that his son, David R. McClain, was Ida Tucker's first husband, Charles D. McLain:

- In 1870 James's estranged wife, "Phebe McLane," age forty, and their apparent twenty-year-old son, "Daniel McLane" (David McLain) lived together in Muskegon[78]—the city where twenty-two-year-old Charles D. McLain married Ida Tucker in 1871. The surname and age of "Daniel" match those of Ida's husband, whose middle initial could have represented *David* or *Daniel*.
- "Daniel" worked in a log boom, catching, sorting, and rafting logs floated down the Muskegon River for the timber industry.[79] The occupation relates to Charles's work as a "Sawyer" in 1871, when he married Ida, and in the "Lumber business" in 1886, when he married Emma.
- David owned carpenter's tools; Ida's husband worked as a carpenter.
- Testimony in the 1879 McLain divorce paints Charles as a self-centered and unreliable man who had alienated his wife and in-laws.[80] Similar traits may underlie David McLain's apparent estrangement from his father in 1885 and his uncle's suing him in 1887.
- Emma's ignorance of Charles's first marriage (as the 1910 census implies) suggests she had little contact with his family, who conceivably knew of both marriages. Emma married Charles about ten months after James died. James's son, David, estranged from his father in 1885, quitclaimed his interest in his father's land before the marriage, and his uncle sued him a few months later. These events may have distanced Emma from her in-laws.
- Like Ida's ex-husband and Emma's husband-to-be, David (or Daniel) McLain seems not to appear in the 1880 census, reducing the likelihood they are different people.
- A divorced couple's children are more likely to divorce than offspring of a successful marriage.[81] Both James McLain and Charles D. McLain divorced.

---

78. 1870 U.S. census, Muskegon Co., Mich., pop. sch., Muskegon, Ward 3, p. 30, dwell. 204, fam. 201, Daniel [David] McLane.

79. Ibid. The enumerator gives Daniel's occupation as "Work Boom," paralleling nearby entries like "Work Mill" and "Engineer Mill." For a description of the log boom's role in the timber industry, see Rector, "Booming," in *Log Transportation in the Lake States Lumber Industry*, 115–46.

80. Allegan Co., Circuit Court file 1355, McLain v. McLain, 1879, Ida M[.] McLain petition for divorce, undated, and affidavits of Etta H. Ganoung, undated, Mrs. Calista J. Tucker, 22 August 1879, and George M. D. Tucker, 22 August 1879. Mrs. Ganoung was Ida's sister; the Tuckers were her parents.

81. Nicholas H. Wolfinger, in "Trends in the Intergenerational Transmission of Divorce," *Demography* 36 (August 1999), 415, reports "numerous researchers have shown that the children of divorces are disproportionately likely to end their own marriages."

Table 3
One Man's Three Identities

IDENTITY	NAMES	BIRTH DATA	OCCUPATIONS	RESIDENCES
Husband and ex-husband of Ida; father of Percy, Leon, and Earl McLain	Charles D. McLain	1848–49 in Michigan	Lumberman Carpenter	Muskegon (city) (1871) Van Buren County (1872–79)
Husband of Emma, father of her children; reported son of James and Mary (née Mapes) McLain	D. McLain Charles D. McLain	1849–62 in Ottawa County, or Kent County Michigan	Lumberman Carpenter	Van Buren County (1886) Newaygo (village) (1886–1925)
Son of James and Phebe (née Wright) McLain	David McLane Daniel McLane David R. McLain	1849–52 in Michigan	Lumberman Carpenter	Kent County (1860, 1886) Muskegon (city) (1870) Newaygo (village) (1886)

CONCLUSION

   Parallel details suggest one Charles D. McLain married (1) Ida Tucker and (2) Emma Cope. Other parallels show that Emma's husband was "David R. McLain," son of James and Phebe (née Wright) McLain. Strengthening the case, in June 1870 Phebe and her son lived in Muskegon, where Charles D. McLain married Ida about fifteen months later. Thus, three identities apparently pertain to one man. James and Phebe were the parents of Charles D. McLain who married Ida Tucker. See table 3. Born probably as David R. McLain, he adopted *Charles* as a first name and used the first letter of his original first name as middle initial. Perhaps estrangement from his father or his parents' separation motivated him to change his name, or he may have wanted more than his middle initial to distinguish himself from his uncle and grandfather named David McLain.

Three Identities of Charles D. McLain of Muskegon, Michigan   119

Records in 1879 and 1886 put Charles in Van Buren County, but his location between those dates is uncertain. On 18 January 1886 David R. McLain was "of Newaygo," apparently the village in Newaygo County. On 4 June 1886, when he quitclaimed his interest in his father's land, David was "of Edgerton," a village in Kent County's Algoma Township, where the tract lay. Perhaps the clerk assumed David lived there, or he may have resided there temporarily. Before 21 October 1886 and as Charles D. McLain, he was back in Newaygo, working and wooing Emma, as her obituary describes. They married across a county line about twenty miles from her home. Like most lumbermen, Charles may have moved along rivers from one stand of trees to another. The residence on his 1886 marriage record—the Van Buren County port of South Haven, on Lake Michigan at the mouth of the Black River—lies about seventy miles from Sparta, where they married. South Haven may technically have been Charles's address in 1886 but not his abode when he was identified as his father's heir, quitclaiming interest in his father's land, and courting Emma.

Charles's birth date also remains uncertain. His first marriage record, the 1870 census, and his death record and obituary place it in 1848–49. In contrast, the 1860 census—the known record closest to his birth—suggests he was born in 1851–52, near the 1853–54 dates his second marriage record and the 1894 and 1900 censuses indicate. If Charles was born in Michigan, as all his records specify, a birth after his father settled there in 1851–52—say in January 1854, as reported in 1900—is correct. If so, he was no older than twenty-one and perhaps as young as sixteen when he married fifteen-year-old Ida, even though they reported their ages as twenty-two and sixteen, respectively.[82] Their youth and the reported hastiness of the marriage may explain its failure.

Common research "efficiencies" initially frustrated recent efforts to find Charles:

- Bypassing records outside the location and timeframe of immediate interest. A census taken almost thirty years after the only Charles D. McLain record known to previous researchers, and a county away, opened a promising research path.
- Not considering variant given names and surnames. "Daniel McLane" lived at the place and time indicated for Ida's groom and he was about the same age, but he did not appear to be Charles D. McLain.
- Overlooking identifying clues beyond a research subject's name. McLain's age, occupations, birthplace and other locations, apparent personality, middle initial, and chronology provide evidence of his identity.

---

82. Muskegon Co., Mich., Record of Marriages 2:36, no. 531, McLain-Tucker, 19 August 1871. Ida married one week before her sixteenth birthday. For her birth date, see Ida Leach family Bible record, family pages only.

- Focusing on one person rather than tracking collateral relatives or using information about them to locate a potentially relevant record or person. Ida's second marriage led to the divorce record and identifying information on her first husband. Pension files of James McLain's brothers and brothers-in-law provide information about James. Information on James McLain identifies his son.

- Not consulting relevant works in which the ancestor will not be named. Helping to identify Charles, a book about the Great Lakes lumber industry describes his "Sawyer" and "Work Boom" occupations. A book on woodworking identifies his tools as those of a carpenter.

Even with attention to the above variables, the early-1970s attempts to locate Ida Tucker's first husband probably could not have succeeded. Three factors explain the difference: indexing, records access, and technology. When Earl McLain's genealogist daughter hired a professional to trace Earl's father, few census indexes existed except those for 1790 and 1880. The latter included only households with children under age ten. Indexes to Michigan's 1870 census, taken the year before Charles and Ida's marriage, did not appear until the 1990s. Although indexed, the 1900 census—which opened up the research this article reports—was inaccessible to researchers until late 1973. The 1910 and 1920 censuses, which corroborate Charles D. McLain's 1900 data, became available in 1983 and 1993, respectively. Without census data, county-by-county searches for Charles in court, land, probate, and vital records would have been untargeted and wide ranging. Although they might eventually have yielded information on David McLain in Kent County and Charles McLain in Newaygo, relevance to Charles McLain of Muskegon would seem doubtful without census data—especially that from 1870 linking Ida's future husband to James McLain's estranged wife. In the early 1970s only line-by-line readings of several counties' enumerations could have led to the pre-1880 census entries this article cites. Even if earlier researchers had undertaken that effort, they probably could not have recognized the useful entries without the benefit of twenty-first-century electronic resources suggesting Emma McLain's husband Charles was James McLain's son David.

In the early 1970s Ida Tucker's first husband probably was untraceable. Today's solution had the advantage of indexing, records access, and technology unavailable a few decades ago. Avoiding the shortcuts enumerated above, the research yielded records seemingly pertinent to three different men. Deductive reasoning shows they apply to one person, revealing Charles D. McLain's origin and history.

Glossary

accurate
A term applied to genealogical sources, information, evidence, and conclusions, and to proof statements, proof summaries, and proof arguments when the GPS shows they portray identities, relationships, and events as they were in the past or are today; compare with *prove*

analysis
Refers to two processes: (*a*) recognizing the information and evidence items a source contains that are likely to answer a research question directly, indirectly, or negatively; (*b*) considering the characteristics, purpose, and history of a source and its relevant information items in order to determine their likely accuracy

authored work
A written product that synthesizes information from many prior sources and presents the writer's own conclusions, interpretations, and thoughts; one of three kinds of genealogical *source*; compare with *record*

bibliography
See *source list*

citation
A source reference that applies a standard format for describing sources

compatible evidence
Independently created research-question answers that agree even if differing in detail (for example, *Molly* and *Mary* may be variants of the same name); the opposite of *conflicting evidence*

conclusion
Refers to two products: (*a*) an answer to a research question that passes tests of analysis and correlation but has not been explained and documented in writing; (*b*) a recapitulation of a proof summary or proof argument that states or restates the proved conclusion

conflicting evidence	Independently created research-question answers that could not all be correct (for example, Molly could not have been born in both Georgia and New York); the opposite of *compatible evidence*
correlation	A process of comparing and contrasting genealogical information and evidence to reveal conflicts, parallels, and patterns
derivative record	A record created from a prior record by (1) transcribing the prior record or part of it by hand, keyboard, or optical-character-recognition, speech-to-text, or other technology, (2) abstracting information from it, (3) translating it from one language to another, or (4) reproducing it with alterations; a work created to expand accessibility to the prior record's information, or to some part of it; the opposite of *original record* and one of three kinds of genealogical *source*; see *record*
direct evidence	An information item that by itself answers a research question; the opposite of *indirect evidence* and one of three categories of genealogical *evidence*
discursive note	A reference note containing discussion, usually along with one or more citations; see *reference note*
document (*verb*)	The processes of recording and showing the sources of concepts, evidence, and words that an author or compiler has used
documentation	The sources supporting genealogical conclusions and proof, citations to those sources, the genealogist's comments about them, and formatting showing the connections between the sources and specific statements and conclusions
endnote	A reference note placed at the end of an article, book, report, Web publication, or other genealogical work to document a statement within the work; see *reference note*; compare with *footnote*
evidence	A research question's tentative answer, which may be right or wrong, complete or incomplete, or vague or specific; may be *direct*, *indirect*, or *negative*

exhaustive search	Research that examines all sources, an impossible task; see *reasonably exhaustive search*
facsimile	An image showing a source with no sign of cropping, blurring, or other alteration; an exact copy; see *image*
first reference note	See *long-form citation*
footnote	A reference note appearing at the bottom of a page to document a statement on that page; see *reference note*; compare with *endnote*
full reference note	See *long-form citation*
Genealogical Proof Standard (GPS)	The genealogy field's standard for differentiating acceptable from unacceptable conclusions
genealogy	A research field concerned primarily with accurately reconstructing forgotten or unknown identities and familial relationships in the past and present, typically covering more than one generation and including adoptive, biological, extramarital, marital, and other kinds of familial relationships; a narrative family history covering descendants of an ancestral couple
GPS	See *Genealogical Proof Standard*
headline style	Capitalization of all words in a group of words except articles, conjunctions, prepositions, and words that are not the group's first or last word [for exceptions, see *The Chicago Manual of Style*, 16th ed. (Chicago: University of Chicago Press, 2010), 448–49)]; the form of capitalization used for formal titles in source citations; compare with *sentence style*
hypothesis	Evidence or a potential conclusion subjected to tests of accuracy; see *evidence* and *conclusion*
identity	Characteristics and contexts distinguishing one person from all other people throughout history
image	A film, photocopy, photograph, scan, video, or other replication of a *physical source*; compare with *facsimile*
independent sources	Sources or information items with unrelated origins that reinforce rather than duplicate each other; the opposite of *related sources*

indeterminable	Refers to information items that cannot be classified as *primary* or *secondary*, because either the informant is unknown or the genealogist cannot deduce how an identified informant obtained the information
indirect evidence	Two or more information items that answer a research question only when combined; the opposite of *direct evidence* and one of three categories of genealogical *evidence*
informant	Someone who provided one or more information items; see *information*
information	Statements based on experience, fabrication, hearsay, intuition, observation, reading, research, or some other means; a source's surface content, including its physical characteristics; what we see or hear when we examine a source, not what we interpret; may be *primary, secondary,* or *indeterminable* (of unknown origin)
long-form citation	A sentence-style format used for a written work's first citation to a particular source and providing all applicable citation details; compare with *short-form citation;* see *citation* and *sentence style*
medium	A means of showing facsimiles or images of physical sources, including digital images, film, microfiche, microfilm, photocopies, photographs, and video; see *facsimile, image,* and *physical source*
negative evidence	A type of evidence arising from an absence of information in extant records where that information might be expected; one of three categories of genealogical *evidence;* compare with *negative search*
negative search	A search that does not yield useful evidence; compare with *negative evidence*
original record	A written report of an action, observation, utterance, or other event, often but not always made at the time of the event or soon after and not based on a prior record; the opposite of *derivative record* and one of three kinds of genealogical *source;* see *record*

physical source	A source viewed via a *medium*; see *source*
primary information	Information about an event provided by an eyewitness to the event; the opposite of *secondary information*
proof	Genealogical data and conclusions that are acceptable because they meet the Genealogical Proof Standard's five criteria
proof argument	A documented narrative explaining why the answer to a complex genealogical problem should be considered acceptable and which may be a stand-alone product, like a case study, journal article, or report, or may appear within a chapter, family history, or other genealogical work in print, online, or elsewhere
proof statement	A documented data item or sentence stating a self-evident acceptable conclusion within a documented genealogical article, blog, chapter, chart, family history, report, table, or other documented work in print, online, or elsewhere
proof summary	A documented narrative or list stating facts that support or lead to an acceptable conclusion and which may be a stand-alone product, may accompany a report or lineage-society application, or may appear in an article, blog, chapter, narrative family history, report, or other genealogical work in print, online, or elsewhere
prove	The process of using the GPS to show that a genealogical information or evidence item, source, or conclusion portrays identities, relationships, and events as they were in the past or are today; to establish that a genealogical conclusion is acceptable
provenance	The history of a source's custody
published source	A source made available for distribution to people wishing a copy; the opposite of *unpublished source*
reasonably exhaustive search	The Genealogical Proof Standard's first element, requiring research thorough enough to meet five criteria: (1) yield at least two independent sources agreeing directly or

indirectly on a research question's answer, (2) cover sources competent genealogists would examine to answer the same research question, (3) provide at least some primary information and direct, indirect, or negative evidence from at least one original record, (4) replace, where possible, relevant authored works, derivative records, and secondary or indeterminable information, and (5) yield data from sources that indexes and databases identify as potentially relevant

record (*noun*) — An account, usually written, of an action, observation, utterance, or other event, typically intended to describe, document, memorialize, or note the action, observation, utterance, or other event; may be *original* or *derivative*; a broad subcategory of genealogical *source*

reference list — See *source list*

reference note — A numbered paragraph-style feature of scholarly writing containing one or more citations documenting a specific fact, statement, or series of statements bearing the same number, superscripted, as the reference note; a generic term covering *footnote* and *endnote*; see *discursive note*

related sources — Sources or information items that can be traced to one informant, source, or origin; therefore items that duplicate, rather than reinforce, each other; the opposite of *independent sources*

relationship — A connection between events, evidence, information, or people

repository — An agency, building, or office housing source material, like an archive (personal, private, or public), courthouse, historical society, library, museum, or town hall, and business, governmental, personal, religious, and other kinds of offices

research — An investigation designed to discover or interpret facts and thus to advance knowledge

research question — A question that research aims to answer; in genealogy a focused question that seeks

	unknown information about a documented person and that helps frame research scope, lead to relevant information, and identify evidence
resolution	The separation of conflicting or incompatible answers to a research question into likely correct and likely incorrect evidence, the discard of the likely incorrect evidence, and the explanation for the separation and rationale(s) for the discarding; see *conflicting evidence*
secondary information	Information reported by someone who obtained it from someone else; hearsay; the opposite of *primary information*
sentence style	Lowercasing all words in a group except the group's first word and any proper nouns, including formal titles, and ending the group with a period; the form of capitalization and punctuation used in citations
short-form citation	A sentence-style format used for all but a work's first citation to a particular source and providing only enough detail to trigger recall and identification of the prior long-form citation and to document the statement to which it is attached; see *long-form citation*
short note	See *short-form citation*
source	A container of information; includes all kinds of publications and unpublished artifacts, records, recordings, and written materials; may be used in a *physical* form or as a *facsimile*
source list	An alphabetical or categorical grouping of citations showing research scope, providing the general documentary basis for the content of a lecture, lesson, presentation, or written work, or directing others to sources related to such content
source-list citation	A paragraph-style format, customarily with a hanging indent, used to identify a source fully but not to document a specific statement, and typically not including reference to a specific item within a source
standard	A principle or measure of quality established by an authority

subsequent note   See *short-form citation*

unpublished source   A source for which only one or a few copies exist,
                         or a source for which distribution is limited to
                         select people or places; the opposite of *published
                         source*

Reading and Source List

Bell, Mary McCampbell. "Finding Original Materials by Using the National Union Catalog of Manuscript Collections." *National Genealogical Society Quarterly* 94 (June 2006): 133–42. [Guide to locating unpublished genealogical sources in archival and historical society collections] [**SLCL**][1]

Board for Certification of Genealogists. *The BCG Genealogical Standards Manual.* Orem, Utah: Ancestry, 2000. [A pioneering work setting out the Genealogical Proof Standard; among seventy-four genealogical standards, it delineates fifty-six research standards. It also provides examples of formatted genealogical reports and compilations meeting those standards.] [**SLCL**]

———. "The Genealogical Proof Standard." *Board for Certification of Genealogists.* http://www.bcgcertification.org/resources/standard.html : 2012. [Identifies the GPS's five elements and explains how each contributes to a research product's credibility]

———. "Skillbuilding." *Board for Certification of Genealogists.* http://www.bcgcertification.org/skillbuilders/index.html : 2012. [Growing collection of electronic versions of articles from the board's newsletter, *OnBoard*, concerning the analysis of many kinds of genealogical sources and providing information about genealogical knowledge, skills, and standards]

The Chicago Manual of Style, 16th edition. Chicago: University of Chicago Press, 2010. [The guide to writing style and documentation that the genealogical field has adopted]

DeGrazia, Laura A. "Skillbuilding: Proof Arguments." *OnBoard: Newsletter of the Board for Certification of Genealogists* 15 (January 2009): 1–3. [Differentiates proof arguments from proof summaries and explains how to develop a proof argument]

---

1. *SLCL* refers to the St. Louis County Library, which holds the NGS Book Loan Collection and makes it available through interlibrary loan. Go to http://www.slcl.org/branches/hq/sc/ngs/ngscol-main.htm to read about the collection and how to borrow materials from it.

Devine, Donn. "Evidence Analysis." In *Professional Genealogy: A Manual for Researchers, Writers, Editors, Lecturers, and Librarians*, ed., Elizabeth Shown Mills. Baltimore: Genealogical Publishing Company, 2001. [Overview of genealogical reasoning and proof] [**SLCL**]

Eakle, Arlene, and Johni Cerny. *The Source: A Guidebook of American Genealogy*. Salt Lake City: Ancestry, 1984. [A guide to American genealogical sources; contains some categories not addressed in the third edition] See Szucs entry below.

Eales, Anne Bruner, and Robert M. Kvasnicka. *Guide to Genealogical Research in the National Archives of the United States*, 3rd edition. Washington, D.C.: National Archives and Records Administration, 2000. [Describes National Archives holdings of greatest value to genealogists] [**SLCL**]

Evans, Stefani. "Data Analysis." *OnBoard: Newsletter of the Board for Certification of Genealogists* 18 (May 2012): 13–14. [A case study demonstrating the process of analysis]

————. "Correlation of Evidence," *OnBoard: Newsletter of the Board for Certification of Genealogists* 18 (September 2012): 21–23. [A case study demonstrating the process of correlation]

Geiger, Linda Woodward. "Guidelines for Evaluating Genealogical Resources." *OnBoard: Newsletter of the Board for Certification of Genealogists* 14 (May 2008): 14–15. [Describes source, information, and evidence categories and the evaluation process]

Greene, David L. "Donald Lines Jacobus, Scholarly Genealogy, and *The American Genealogist*." *The American Genealogist* 72 (July/October 1997): 159–80. [Review of the development of a scientific approach to genealogical research] [**SLCL**]

Greenwood, Val D. *The Researcher's Guide to American Genealogy*, 3rd edition. Baltimore: Genealogical Publishing Company, 2000. [A detailed guide to American genealogical records and research] See especially the chapters on "Understanding Genealogical Research," "Analyzing the Pedigree and the Place," "Evaluation of Evidence," and "Organizing and Evaluating Research Findings." [**SLCL**]

Hait, Michael. *Online State Resources for Genealogy*, e-book in PDF format, 2nd edition. Privately published, 2012. [Descriptions of state, county, and local records of genealogical value made available online by governmental agencies, libraries, and museums in all fifty states]

Jones, Thomas W. "A Conceptual Model of Genealogical Evidence: Linkage between Present-Day Sources and Past Facts." *National Genealogical Society Quarterly* 86 (March 1998): 5–18. [Describes genealogical evidence as a mental construct] [**SLCL**]

———. "Essential Elements of Genealogical Documentation." *The Journal of the Cape Cod Genealogical Society* 2 (June 2012): 94–99. [Describes key resources for genealogical documentation, what to document, where to document, and essential source-citation elements]

———. "Focused Versus Diffuse Research." *OnBoard: Newsletter of the Board for Certification of Genealogists* 17 (September 2011): 17–18. [Explains how focused research is more efficient and effective than other approaches]

———. "The Genealogical Proof Standard: How Simple Can It Be?" *OnBoard: Newsletter of the Board for Certification of Genealogists* 16 (September 2010): 17–18 and 20. [Uses a straightforward case study to demonstrate the GPS]

———. "How Much Searching is 'Reasonably Exhaustive'?" *Association of Professional Genealogists Quarterly* 25 (March 2010): 25–33. [Explains the criteria for the reasonably exhaustive search and provides guidelines for research planning]

———. "Models for Proving Parentage," lecture material. In *Passages Through Time: September 2–5, 2009*; Little Rock, Arkansas, conference syllabus on CD-ROM. Austin, Texas: Federation of Genealogical Societies, 2009. Pages 164–67, session Th-72. [Describes eight models for assembling genealogical evidence into a conclusion for proof]

———. "The Road Less Traveled: The Power of Indirect Evidence." *Association of Professional Genealogists Quarterly* 20 (March 2005): 21–26. [Explains indirect evidence and provides examples showing how using indirect evidence can break through genealogical brick walls]

———. "Perils of Source Snobbery." *OnBoard: Newsletter of the Board for Certification of Genealogists* 19 (May 2012): 9–10 and 15. [Shows how using disdained sources can help advance genealogical research projects and how blindly trusting preferred sources can create barriers]

———. "What is the Standard of Proof in Genealogy?" *NGS NewsMagazine* 33 (April/May/June 2007): 22–26. [An overview of the GPS]

Leary, Helen F. M. "Evidence Revisited—DNA, POE, and GPS." *OnBoard: Newsletter of the Board for Certification of Genealogists* 4 (January 1998): 1–2 and 5. [A classic article introducing the Genealogical Proof Standard]

————. "Problem Analyses and Research Plans." In *Professional Genealogy: A Manual for Researchers, Writers, Editors, Lecturers, and Librarians*, ed., Elizabeth Shown Mills. Baltimore: Genealogical Publishing Company, 2001. [Definitive guide to analyzing genealogical problems and planning research to address them] [**SLCL**]

Leary, Helen F. M., Elizabeth Shown Mills, and Christine Rose. "Evidence Analysis." In *1999 NGS Conference in the States: Richmond, Virginia*, program syllabus. Arlington, Va.: National Genealogical Society, 1999. [A ground-breaking effort focused on the evaluation and use of sources, information, and evidence]

LeClerc, Michael J., and Henry B. Hoff. *Genealogical Writing in the 21st Century: A Guide to Register Style and More*, 2nd edition. Boston: New England Historic Genealogical Society, 2006. [A guide to preparing genealogies for publication] [**SLCL**]

Little, Barbara Vines. "Skillbuilding: It's Not That Hard to Write Proof Arguments." *OnBoard: Newsletter of the Board for Certification of Genealogists* 15 (September 2009): 20–23. [Explains the differences between proof summaries and arguments and the uses of each]

Macy, Harry, Jr. "Recognizing Scholarly Genealogy and Its Importance to Genealogists and Historians." *New England Historical and Genealogical Register* 150 (January 1996): 7–28. [Overview of American genealogy's development as a scholarly discipline] [**SLCL**]

Mathews, Barbara Jean. "Reporting on a Brick Wall: The Genealogical Travelogue." *Association of Professional Genealogists Quarterly* 17 (December 2002): 131.

Merriman, Brenda Dougall. *Genealogical Standards of Evidence: A Guide for Family Historians*. Toronto: Dundurn Press, 2010. [Overview of genealogical standards with many examples illustrating their application] [**SLCL**]

Mills, Elizabeth Shown. *Evidence! Citation and Analysis for the Family Historian*. Baltimore: Genealogical Publishing: 1997. [Groundbreaking guide to genealogical analysis and citation; largely superseded by *Evidence Explained*] [[**SLCL**]

————. *Evidence Explained: Historical Analysis, Citation, and Source Usage*. https://www.evidenceexplained.com/ : 2012. [Website with forums and lessons on genealogical reasoning and source citation] See especially "QuickLesson 1: Analysis & Citation ," "QuickLesson 2: Sources vs. Information vs. Evidence vs. Proof," "QuickLesson 8: What Constitutes Proof?," and "QuickLesson 10: Original Records, Image Copies, and Derivatives."

Mills, Elizabeth Shown. *Evidence Explained: Citing History Sources from Artifacts to Cyberspace,* 2nd edition, revised. Baltimore: Genealogical Publishing Company, 2009. Also, digital edition, 2012, *Evidence Explained: Historical Analysis, Citation, and Source Usage* (https://www.evidenceexplained.com/ : accessed 1 August 2012), via "Book Store." [The genealogy field's comprehensive guide to source citation, organized by source categories] See especially the first two chapters, "Fundamentals of Evidence Analysis" and "Fundamentals of Citation." [**SLCL**]

————. "Genealogy in the 'Information Age': History's New Frontier?" *National Genealogical Society Quarterly* 91 (December 2003): 260–77. [Reviews the history of genealogy as a discipline and offers rationales for its academic legitimacy] [**SLCL**]

————. "Research Reports" and "Proof Arguments and Case Studies." In *Professional Genealogy: A Manual for Researchers, Writers, Editors, Lecturers, and Librarians,* ed., Elizabeth Shown Mills. Baltimore: Genealogical Publishing Company, 2001. [Detailed guides to organizing and writing articles, case studies, proof arguments and reports] Besides Mills's chapters, see the Devine and Leary chapters cited above. [**SLCL**]

————. "Working with Historical Evidence: Genealogical Principles and Standards." *National Genealogical Society Quarterly* 87 (September 1999): 165–84. [Reviews the evolution of the Genealogical Proof Standard and describes it; explains four ways to assemble evidence to achieve genealogical proof] [**SLCL**]

Rose, Christine. *Genealogical Proof Standard: Building a Solid Case,* 3rd edition. San Jose, Calif.: CR Publications, 2009. [An introduction to the Genealogical Proof Standard] [**SLCL**]

Ross-Larson, Bruce. *Edit Yourself: A Manual for Everyone Who Works with Words,* 2nd edition. New York: W. W. Norton, 1996. [A guide to writing concisely and clearly]

Rubincam, Milton, ed. *Genealogical Research: Methods and Sources,* vol. 1, 2nd edition. Washington D.C.: American Society of Genealogists, 1980. [In-depth guide to American genealogical methods and materials, organized geographically and for "Pre-American Ancestry"] [**SLCL**]

"Rubrics for Evaluating New Applications for BCG Certification," PDF. *Board for Certification of Genealogists.* http://www.bcgcertification .org/certification/judging.html. [Provides criteria for evaluating genealogical products claiming to meet the Genealogical Proof Standard]

Sayre, Pamela Boyer. "Effective Writing and Editing." *OnBoard: Newsletter of the Board for Certification of Genealogists* 16 (September 2010): 21–22. [Describes and recommends print and online guides to writing proficiently]

Stevenson, Noel C. *Genealogical Evidence: A Guide to the Standard of Proof Relating to Pedigrees, Ancestry, Heirship, and Family History.* Laguna Hills, Calif.: Aegean Park, 1979. [A classic guide, from a legal perspective, to using genealogical evidence and reasoning by category of genealogical source] [**SLCL**]

―――. "The Rules of Evidence: A Standard for Proving Pedigrees." In *Genealogical Research: Methods and Sources*, vol. 1, 2nd edition, ed., Milton Rubincam. Washington D.C.: American Society of Genealogists, 1980. [Classic description of a standard of proof for genealogists] [**SLCL**]

Stratton, Eugene Aubrey. *Applied Genealogy.* Salt Lake City: Ancestry, 1988. [In-depth discussions of a range of genealogical topics] See especially the chapters on "Analyzing Evidence" and "Indirect Evidence." [**SLCL**]

Strunk, William, Jr., and E. B. White. *The Elements of Style.* 1935. Revised edition; New York: Macmillan, 1962. [A classic guide to writing clearly and concisely] [**SLCL**]

Szucs, Loretto Dennis, and Sandra Hargreaves Luebking. *The Source: A Guidebook to American Genealogy*, 3rd edition. Provo, Utah: Ancestry, 2006. [A guide to American genealogical sources; updates and expands some of the first edition's categories and contains some categories that the first edition does not address] See Eakle and Cerny entry above. [**SLCL**]

Answers to exercises

Chapter 1 exercise answers

1. What is genealogy?

   Genealogy is a research field concerned primarily with accurately reconstructing forgotten or unknown identities and familial relationships in the past and present, typically covering more than one generation and including adoptive, biological, extramarital, marital, and other kinds of familial relationships.

2. What are the GPS's five elements?

   1. *Thorough ("reasonably exhaustive") searches in sources that might help reliably answer a research question*

   2. *Informative ("complete, accurate") citations to the sources of every information item contributing to the research question's answer*

   3. *Analysis and comparison ("correlation") of the relevant sources and information items to assess their usefulness as evidence of the research question's answer*

   4. *Resolution of any conflicts between evidence and the proposed answer to the research question*

   5. *A written statement, list, or narrative supporting the answer*

3. You have shared your family history with someone who wants you to omit all the proof statements, proof summaries, and proof arguments, including explanations of reasoning and documentation. How do you reply?

   Without explanations of reasoning and documentation, accuracy is unknown. Only documented proof statements, proof summaries, proof arguments, and explanations of reasoning show that a compilation likely is accurate and trustworthy. Also, by showing that our work meets the Genealogical Proof Standard, we create work that will be useful for generations to come.

4. Why can't a genealogical conclusion be partially proved?

Because the GPS's five parts are interdependent

5. What is the first step in genealogical research?

To ask questions about a documented person's unknown relationships or other information we want to learn about that person.

Chapter 2 exercise answers

1. Read the article in appendix A and identify the major question the research was designed to answer.

   Who were the parents of Philip Pritchett who died in Montgomery County, Kentucky, in 1811–12?

2. List two other questions in the same article that the reported research answers.

   Where did Philip live when he sued Moses Baker?

   Where was Lewis Pritchett of Fairfax County born?

   Who were the parents of Lewis Pritchett of Fairfax County?

   [Many other questions also would be correct answers to this exercise.]

3. Read the article in appendix B and identify the major question or questions the research was designed to answer.

   Who were the parents of Charles D. McLain who married Ida May Tucker in Muskegon, Michigan, in 1871, and what became of him after their divorce?

4. List two other questions in the same article that the reported research answers.

   Did Ida May Tucker and Emma Cope marry the same man?

   Did Emma Cope marry Charles D. McLain or David R. McLain?

   Was Phebe Wright or Mary Mapes the mother of Charles aka David McLain?

   [Many other questions also would be correct answers to this exercise.]

5. Using this chapter's criteria for effective research questions . . . , write three relationship research questions . . . for research you plan to undertake.

   Your questions will seek information about a documented person's relatives, such as the person's parents, children, or spouse. Your questions will be neither too broad nor too narrow, and they will include no unsupportable assumptions.

6. Using this chapter's criteria for effective research questions, write an identity research question . . . for research you plan to undertake.

   Your question will seek information about a documented person's identity—a characteristic distinguishing the person from other people, especially those who might have the same name. Your question will be neither too broad nor too narrow, and it will include no unsupportable assumptions.

7. Using this chapter's criteria for effective research questions, write an activity research question . . . for research you plan to undertake.

   Your question will seek information about an activity or event in which a documented person may have participated. Your question will be neither too broad nor too narrow, and it will include no unsupportable assumptions.

8. List four authored works (not derivative records) cited in the articles in appendixes A and B.

   Willis M. Kemper, *Genealogy of the Kemper Family* . . . (appendix A, note 7)

   Donn Devine, *"The Common Law of England"* . . . (appendix A, note 36)

   Thomas W. Jones, *"Merging Identities Properly"* . . . (appendix B, note 1)

   William Gerald Rector, *"Loggers and Logging"* . . . (appendix B, note 7)

[Other examples appear in appendix B, notes 16, 27–29, and 81, and table 2.]

9. List four original records cited in the article in appendix A.

   1810 U.S. census, Montgomery Co., Ky. (note 3)

   Tax Books, Clark Co., Ky. (note 4)

   Personal Property Tax Lists, Fauquier Co., Va. (note 7)

   Fairfax Co., Order Book 1788–92 (note 15)

   [Many other sources also would be correct answers to this item.]

10. List four derivative records cited in the article in appendix A.

    Schreiner-Yantis and Love, *The 1787 Census of Virginia* (note 9; derived from tax records)

    Mitchell, *Fairfax County Road Orders* (note 18; derived from the original handwritten orders)

King, comp., *The Register of Overwharton Parish* (note 26; derived from the original register)

Peters, *The Tax Man Cometh* (note 32; derived from handwritten lists in the county's papers)

11. Explain why you would prefer an original record containing primary information over a derivative record containing secondary information.

    Original records containing primary information will have fewer errors than derivative sources containing secondary information.

12. Suppose you find an entry of interest in "California Birth Index, 1905–1995," on *Ancestry.com* (http://search.ancestry.com/search/db.aspx?dbid =5247&enc=1). What should be your next step?

    Order a copy of the birth certificate, which will be more reliable and provide more information.

13. Follow the model in the table and list elements of three additional primary information items and three secondary information items with identified informants in the article in appendix B.

INFORMATION ITEM	TYPE	SOURCE	INFORMANT
Ida's husband was a carpenter	*Primary*	*Testimony in circuit court case file (note 12)*	*Calista J. Tucker, Ida's mother*
Ida married young because she envied her older sister	*Secondary*	*Interview by author (note 2)*	*Bernice Turner, Ida's daughter*
Ida had five children after Earl	*Primary*	*Ida's family Bible record (note 3)*	*Ida*
Charles was subpoenaed in Van Buren County	*Primary*	*The subpoena in the circuit court file (note 13)*	*Sheriff William Ray*
Charles died at age seventy-six years, two months, and twenty days	*Secondary*	*Charles's death record (note 23)*	*Probably Charles's widow or daughter*
James McLain was born in July 1827	*Primary*	*Mary McLain affidavit in Stewart J. McLain pension application file (note 36)*	*James's mother*
James McLain died on 7 and 16 December 1885 (two separate information items)	*Secondary*	*Margieanna McLain affidavits in her Civil War pension application file (note 66)*	*James's estranged widow*

[Many other information items could be correct answers to this exercise.]

14. In the following table list three additional information items from the article in appendix A that the author uses as direct evidence. Follow the example to fill in the following for each item: its source, the question the evidence answers, and the answer it gives.

INFORMATION ITEM	SOURCE	QUESTION	ANSWER
Naming "Alpherd" and Lewis among "all my children"	*Will Book A:106–7*	*Who were Philip's children?*	*"Alpherd," Lewis, and others unnamed*
Philip paid taxes in Fairfax County in 1786–93	*tax books* *(note 10)*	*Where did Philip live?*	*In Fairfax County*
The heirs of Lewis Pritchett of Fairfax County sold Stafford County land he had owned	*Stafford Co., Deed Book MM:338* *(note 24)*	*Was Lewis of Fairfax County also Lewis Pritchett the absentee Stafford Co. landlord?*	*Yes*
Lewis Pritchett, son of Lewis and Mary, was christened in Stafford County in 1748	*Register of Overwharton Parish* *(note 26)*	*Who were the parents of Lewis Pritchett born before 1756?*	*Lewis and Mary*

[Many other information items could be correct answers to this exercise.]

15. In the following table list three additional sets of information items from the article in appendix A that the author uses together as indirect evidence. Follow the example to fill in the following for each set of items: its source or sources, the question the evidence answers, and the answer it gives.

INFORMATION ITEMS	SOURCES	QUESTIONS	ANSWER
Philip Pritchett paid Kentucky taxes in 1797; as a minor he sued in Fauquier County in 1783 with "next friend" Lewis Pritchett. The Kentucky Philip was over age 45 in 1810, he had a son Lewis, and his executor came from Fauquier County.	The sources cited in appendix A, notes 4 and 6–8	Was the adult Philip Pritchett in Kentucky the minor in the Virginia lawsuit?	Yes
The only Philip Pritchett taxpayer in Virginia after the lawsuit lived in Fairfax County, which adjoins Fauquier, and where he associated with a Lewis Pritchett, who had the same name as the "next friend" in the lawsuit. This Philip, born about 1765, would have been a minor at the time of the lawsuit	The sources cited in footnotes 9–18 and in figure 1	Was Philip of Fairfax County the complainant in the Fauquier County trespass suit?	Yes
Two Lewis Pritchetts paid tax on land in Stafford County, but only one man of that name paid personal property taxes.	The land and personal property tax lists cited in footnotes 19–21 and table 1.	Was Lewis Pritchett, the owner of land in Stafford County, an absentee landlord?	Yes
Trespasser Moses Baker lived closer to Stafford County than Fairfax County. Philip was in Stafford County in 1781, two years before the lawsuit. A minor's parents often serve as his next friend. The only viable candidate for Philip's father lived in Stafford County in 1783.	The sources cited in figure 1 and in notes 35–36.	Who represented Philip in the 1783 Fauquier County lawsuit?	Philip's father, Lewis Pritchett (not Philip's brother of that name)

16. In the table below, list two or more additional absence-of-information items from the article in appendix A that the author uses as negative evidence. Follow the example to fill in the following for each item: its source, the question the evidence answers, and the answer it gives.

ABSENCE-OF-INFORMATION ITEM	SOURCE	QUESTION	ANSWER
Philip did not pay taxes in Fauquier County.	*Tax lists (note 13)*	*Did Philip live in Fauquier County?*	*No*
Philip did not pay taxes in Fairfax County before 1786.	*Tax lists (notes 10 and 14)*	*When was Philip born?*	*About 1765*
Heirs of Lewis Pritchett of Fairfax County include no Philip.	*List of heirs (note 29)*	*Was Lewis Pritchett of Fairfax Philip's father?*	*No*

17. Explain why one of your answers to question 15 is an example of indirect evidence and not direct evidence.

    Because one source or information item does not answer the question all by itself. The answer appears only by combining the information items and understanding (inferring) what they mean together.

18. Explain why one of your answers to question 16 is an example of negative evidence and not direct evidence.

    Because an absence of specific information in a source where it might be expected answers the question.

Chapter 3 exercise answers

1. The research reported in appendix A addresses the research question *When was Philip Pritchett born?* and the article gives the answer *about 1763.* (See the article's page 38, first paragraph under "Conclusion.") How does the conclusion *Philip Pritchett was born about 1763* meet the six criteria for a reasonably exhaustive search? To answer this question, give specific examples from the article and its documentation for each of the following criteria:

   a. At least two independent evidence items in agreement

   The 1810 census (note 3), the 1783 court appearance as a minor (notes 6 and 8), and the first tax-list appearance in 1786 (notes 10 and 14) agree that Philip was born between 1762 and 1765.

   b. All sources competent genealogists would examine.

   Few birth or baptismal records exist for this time and place, and those that are known do not name Philip. Of censuses, only that for 1810 survives for the time and places he lived. Only the sources listed under item a above and a legislative petition (note 35) are known to give evidence of Philip's age or birth date.

   c. Some primary information

   The court record, tax list, and petition offer primary information. The informant for the census is unknown.

   d. Some original records

   All the sources mentioned are original records.

   e. Relevant derivative sources or secondary information replaced by findable corresponding originals and primary information

   The derivative record for the 1787 tax list (note 9) was replaced by viewing the original tax list on microfilm (note 10).

f. All findable sources suggested by relevant sources and indexes

A census index and database led to an image of the original census page. Other derivative sources led to the court record and petition.

2. After the research reported in appendix B was published, a student discovered that the 1850 U.S. census of Mercer County, Ohio, includes the household of "Jas McLean," 23, apparent wife Phebe, 22, child Sarah, 5, and no one else. They lived near the parents and brother of Phebe (Wright) McLain. This finding requires reconsidering the article's answer to the question *When was James and Phebe's son David born?* (summarized on the article's page 119, paragraph 2). The new evidence (negative evidence, since David is not enumerated) eliminates the three sources giving evidence of his pre-1850 birth, leaving the new finding and other sources supporting a new answer, *between 1850 and 1854.* How does this new conclusion meet the six criteria for a reasonably exhaustive search? To answer this question give specific examples from the article, its documentation, and the new finding for each of the following criteria:

a. At least two independent evidence items in agreement

David aka Charles's 1886 marriage record to Emma Cope giving the groom's age as thirty-two (note 21) and the 1894 Michigan census giving Emma's husband's age as forty (table 1, note a) agree he was born in 1853–54.

b. All sources competent genealogists would examine

The 1850 census (mentioned above) implies he was born after the enumeration or visitation date. The censuses for 1860 (note 48), 1870 (note 78), and 1894–1920 (table 1, notes a–d) give his age.

Both his marriage records (notes 6 and 21) give his age.

His obituary (note 22) gives his birth date

His death record gives his age at death (note 23).

c. Some primary information

Charles likely provided the age information for his marriage records, making it primary information (He would know his age from experience, but not his exact birth date.)

d. Some original records

All the sources mentioned above, except the 1870 census and perhaps a few other censuses, are original sources.

e. Relevant authored works, derivative records, and secondary information replaced by findable corresponding originals and primary information

Besides the information Charles provided for his marriage records, primary information of his age or birth date is not known to exist. The original 1870 census and the originals of any other cited hand-copied censuses are not known to exist.

f. All findable sources suggested by relevant sources and indexes

Census, death, and marriage indexes and databases are replaced by images of the census pages and other records.

3. Suppose you are researching Mary L. Jones, who appears in the Silas Jones and Sarah E. Jones household in the 1860 U.S. census of Hamilton County, Illinois. Your research question is *Who were Mary's parents?* Using the Family History Library catalog (https://www.familysearch .org/#form=catalog) and any other resources you wish, list finding aids and sources you might use to pursue answers to your research question. Single out at least two original records likely to provide primary information about Mary's parentage.

   Indexes to the 1860 U.S. census referenced in the question and other censuses might show Mary in a parental household. Some of these censuses are original records, but the informant would be unknown.

   Hamilton County, Illinois, probate files are indexed on FHL microfilm 988,220. A will or estate record for Silas would likely name his widow (if any) and children. This would be an original record and primary information.

   Hamilton County probate journals and will records (images available on the FamilySearch website) are browsable, not searchable, but they include the clerk's handwritten index at the front of each volume. An estate record for Silas would likely name his widow (if any) and children. This would be an original record containing primary information.

   Originals of the Hamilton County marriage records are available only at the Hamilton County courthouse, but the Family History Library catalog lists several books derived from those records.

   • *If Mary married in Hamilton County, her marriage license application could name her parents. This would be primary information. The original record could be viewed at the courthouse.*

   • *If Silas married in Hamilton County, the date and bride's name would give evidence that she was or was not Mary's mother. This would be primary information and, if viewed at the courthouse, it would be in an original record.*

Images of index cards to the Civil War pension application files are on Ancestry.com and Fold3.com. Silas may have served in the war. If he died during the war, the file—an original record—is likely to provide primary information naming his widow and children. If he survived the war, the file may include a form he filled out naming his offspring and providing their birth dates. This also would be primary information.

A database of Illinois death certificates is online at FamilySearch.org and the Illinois State Archives website, but the original certificate would need to be viewed on Family History Library microfilm or purchased as a photocopy from the Illinois Department of Health. If the microfilm or photocopy names Mary's parents, this likely would be secondary information in an original record.

Chapter 4 exercise answers

1. Why should genealogists cite sources completely and accurately?

   The most important use of citations is to support genealogical proof statements, summaries, and arguments. Citations show that our research scope was "reasonably exhaustive." Citations' components and formats—sometimes along with narrative discussion—show that our conclusions rest on the least error-prone sources available. Citations also document our findings and explanations.

   [Chapter 4 exercise answers continue on next page.]

2. Following the model, place in the table the elements of five additional reference-note citations to published sources from the article in appendixes A and B:

   a.   Appendix A, note 7, the last citation

   b.   Appendix A, note 8, the last citation

   c.   Appendix A, note 36, the last citation

   d.   Appendix B, note 24, the last citation

   e.   Appendix B, note 28

   f.   Appendix B, note 70, the last citation

WHO?	WHAT?	WHEN?	WHERE IS?	WHERE IN?
a. Willis M. Kemper	*Genealogy of the Kemper Family . . .*	1899	Chicago: Geo. K. Hazlitt	page 79
b. Anne Bruner Eales and Robert M. Kvasnicka	*Guide to Genealogical Research in the National Archives of the United States*	2000	Washington, D.C.: National Archives and Records Administration	page 23
c. Donn Devine	"The Common Law of England," *NGS Quarterly* 95	September 2007	[not applicable]	pages 165–78, quotation from page 168
d. [not provided]	"Rites Held on Sunday for Mrs. Emma McLain, Long-time Local Resident," *Newaygo Republican*	18 March 1948	Newaygo, Mich.	page 1, column 4
e. DeWayne G. Baker, comp.	"Ancestry World Tree Project: Baker Odyssey," *Ancestry .com*	17 January 2008 [See note preceding footnote 1.]	http://awt.ancestry.com	
f. Denise Crawford	"Descendants of Aaron McClain and Elizabeth\Ann (—)," *Pedigree Resource File,* CD-ROM 18	2000	Salt Lake City: Church of Jesus Christ of Latter-day Saints	[not provided]

3. Convert the same six long-form reference-note citations to short-form reference-note citations.

   a. Kemper, *Genealogy of the Kemper Family*, 79.

   b. Eales and Kvasnicka, *Guide to Genealogical Research*, 23.

   c. Devine, "The Common Law," 168.

   d. "Rites Held on Sunday."

   e. Baker, comp., "Baker Odyssey."

   f. Crawford, "Descendants of Aaron McLain."

   [Several variants of the above also would be correct answers.]

4. Convert the same six long-form reference-note citations to source-list citations.

   a. Kemper, Willis M. *Genealogy of the Kemper Family: Descendants of John Kemper of Virginia*. Chicago: Geo. K. Hazlitt, 1899.

   b. Eales, Ann Bruner, and Robert M. Kvasnicka. *Guide to Genealogical Research in the National Archives of the United States*. Washington, D.C.: National Archives and Records Administration, 2000.

   c. Devine, Donn. "The Common Law of England." *NGS Quarterly* 95 (September 2007).

   d. *Newaygo Republican*. Newaygo, Michigan.

   e. Baker, DeWayne G., comp. "Ancestry World Tree Project: Baker Odyssey." *Ancestry.com*. htttp://awt.ancestry.com : 2008.

   f. Crawford, Denise. "Descendants of Aaron McClain and Elizabeth\Ann (—)." *Pedigree Resource File*, CD-ROM 18. Salt Lake City: Church of Jesus Christ of Latter-day Saints, 2000.

   [Several variants of the above also would be correct answers.]

[Chapter 4 exercise answers continue on next page.]

5. Following the model, place in the table the elements of five additional reference-note citations to unpublished sources:

    a.   Appendix A, note 4, first citation

    b.   Appendix A, note 6

    c.   Appendix A, note 16

    d.   Appendix A, note 25 (ignoring the microfilm)

    e.   Appendix B, note 6 (ignoring the microfilm)

    f.   Appendix B, notes 11–12 (ignoring the microfilm)

WHO?	WHAT?	WHEN?	WHERE IN?	WHERE IS?
a. Kentucky Tax Assessor	Tax Books, Clark Co.	1793–1797, 1799–1809	1795, 6:25; and 1796, 2:21	Kentucky Historical Society, Frankfort
b. Fauquier Co.	Minute Book	1781–84	page 192	County Court, Warrenton, Va.
c. Fairfax Co.	Record of Surveys	1790 (noted in the text)	page 154	Circuit Court Archives, Fairfax, Va.
d. [not provided]	Legislative Petitions, Virginia General Assembly, Stafford Co.	1776–1827	petition of 15 October 1776	record group 78, box 238, folder 1, accession 36121, Library of Virginia, Richmond
e. Muskegon Co., Mich.	Record of Marriages 2	19 August 1871	page 36, no. 531, McLain-Tucker	County Clerk, Muskegon, Mich.
f. Allegan Co., Mich.	Circuit Court File 1355, Ida M. McLain v. Charles D. McLain, 1879	22 August 1879	Mrs. Calista J. Tucker testimony	Circuit Court, Allegan, Mich.

6. Convert the same six long-form reference-note citations to short-form reference-note citations.

    a. Kentucky Tax Assessor, Tax Books, Clark Co., 1795, 6:25; and 1795, 2:21.

    b. Fauquier Co., Minute Book, 1781–84, p. 192.

    c. Fairfax Co., Record of Surveys, p. 154.

    d. Legislative Petitions, Stafford Co., petition of 15 October 1776.

    e. Muskegon Co., Record of Marriages 2:36.

    f. Allegan Co., Circuit Court File 1355, Calista J. Tucker testimony.

[Several variants of the above also would be correct answers.]

7. Convert the same six long-form reference-note citations to source-list citations.

    a. Kentucky Tax Assessor. Tax Books, Clark Co. Kentucky Historical Society, Frankfort, Ky.

    b. Virginia. Fauquier Co. Minute Book, 1781–84. County Court, Warrenton.

    c. Virginia. Fairfax Co. Record of Surveys. Circuit Court Archives, Fairfax.

    d. Legislative Petitions, Virginia Assembly, Stafford Co. Record group 78. Library of Virginia, Richmond.

    e. Michigan. Muskegon Co. Record of Marriages. County Clerk, Muskegon.

    f. Allegan Co. Circuit Court files. Circuit Court, Allegan.

[Several variants of the above also would be correct answers.]

8. Suppose you quote a sentence on page 35 of this chapter. Write a long-form reference-note citation documenting the quotation's source.

Thomas W. Jones, *Mastering Genealogical Proof* (Arlington, Va.: National Genealogical Society, 2013), 35.

9. Write a long-form reference-note citation to any journal or magazine article. If you read the article online, write the citation as if you read the physical journal or magazine.

Warren C. Pratt, "Finding the Father of Henry Pratt of Southeastern Kentucky," *National Genealogical Society Quarterly* 100 (June 2012): 85–103.

10. Search *Find A Grave* for George Tucker in Antrim County, Michigan. Click through to the page containing the "Memorial." Cite it with a long-form reference-note citation.

> DRBUCK, contributor, "George Moore Davis Tucker," memorial 40735875, *Find A Grave* (http://www.findagrave.com/index.html : viewed 1 August 2012).

11. Write a long-form reference-note citation for the Web page at http://www.bcgcertification.org/resources/standard.html.

> "The Genealogical Proof Standard," *Board for Certification of Genealogists* (http://www.bcgcertification.org/resources/standard .html : viewed 1 August 2012).

12. Following the model, separate each of the following double reference-note citations into its two parts and fill in the following table with each part's citation elements.

> a. Board for Certification of Genealogists, *The BCG Genealogical Standards Manual* (Orem: Utah: Ancestry, 2000), 1–2; digital images (incomplete), *Google Books* (http://books.google.com/books?id=I0Eg VqgKp6oC&printsec=frontcover&source=gbs_ge_summary_r&cad=0 #v=onepage&q&f=false : viewed 1 August 2012).

> b. Van Buren Co., Mich., Return of Births in the County of Van Buren for the Year Ending December 31st, A.D. 1876, p. 256, no. 890, Carl McLain, 4 February; Department of Vital Records; Lansing; digital image, "Michigan Births, 1867–1902," *FamilySearch* (https://familysearch.org/pal:/MM9.3.1/TH-267-12877-145173-47?cc=1459684 : viewed 1 August 2012).

> c. "List of all Passengers in Vessels from Foreign Ports Which Have Arrived at the Port of New Orleans during the Third Quarter of the Year 1832—and the Number That Have Died on the Passage," in *Quarterly Abstracts of Passenger Lists of Vessels Arriving at New Orleans, 1820–1875*, microfilm publication M272, 17 rolls (Washington, D.C.: National Archives and Records Service, 1969), roll 1, chronologically arranged, for "Brig Wm Osborne," 3 July 1832, Merdet entries; digital image, "New Orleans, Passenger List Quarterly Abstracts, 1820–1875," *Ancestry.com* (http://www.ancestry.com : downloaded 1 August 2012), search for "G Merdet."

WHO?	WHAT?	WHEN?	WHERE IS?	WHERE IN?
a1. Board for Certification of Genealogists	*The BCG Genealogical Standards Manual*	2000	Orem, Utah: Ancestry	pages 1–2
a2. [not applicable; creator has same name as title]	*Google Books*	1 August 2012	http://books.google.com/books?id=I0EgVqgKp6oC&printsec=frontcover&source=gbs_ge_summary_r&cad=0#v=onepage&q&f=false	
b1. Van Buren Co., Mich.	Return of Births in the County of Van Buren for the Year Ending December 31st, A.D. 1876	4 February 1876	Department of Vital Records; Lansing	p. 256, no. 890, Carl McLain
b2. [not needed]	"Michigan Births, 1867–1902," *FamilySearch*	1 August 2012	https://familysearch.org/pal:/MM9.3.1/TH-267-12877-145173-47?cc=1459684	
c1. [not applicable]	"List of all Passengers in Vessels from Foreign Ports Which Have Arrived at the Port of New Orleans During the Third Quarter of the Year 1832—and the Number That Have Died on the Passage," in *Quarterly Abstracts of Passenger Lists of Vessels Arriving at New Orleans, 1820–1875,* microfilm publication M272, 17 rolls	1969	Washington, D.C.: National Archives and Records Service	roll 1, chronologically arranged, for "Brig Wm Osborne," 3 July 1832, Merdet entries
c2. [not applicable]	"New Orleans, Passenger List Quarterly Abstracts, 1820-1875," *Ancestry.com*	1 August 2012	http://www.ancestry.com	search for "G Merdet."

13. If you do not have an account at *FamilySearch* create one at https://ident
.familysearch.org/cis-web/pages/registration/registration.html and sign
in. Then write a double long-form reference-note citation documenting
the physical source and digital image at https://familysearch.org/pal:/
MM9.3.1/TH-566-11216-4918-97?cc=1320969.

> Georgia Bureau of Vital Statistics, Standard Certificate of Death, no.
> 16678, for John Thomas Wright, 18 May 1923; Georgia Department
> of Archives and History, Morrow; digital image, "Historical Record
> Collections," *FamilySearch* (https://familysearch.org/pal:/MM9.3.1/
> TH-566-11216-4918-97?cc=1320969 : downloaded 1 August 2012),
> for "Georgia, Deaths, 1914–1927," digital folder 004178242, image
> 213.

14. Sign in at *FamilySearch*, and then write a double long-form reference-note
citation documenting the physical source and digital image at https://
familysearch.org/pal:/MM9.3.1/TH-1951-21742-22837-88?cc=1447
693&wc=12205332

> Aroostook Co., Maine, Southern Registry, Deed Book 51:98, Jewell to
> Mansur, 22 January 1875; County Clerk, Holton, Maine; digital image,
> "Historical Record Collections," *FamilySearch* (https://familysearch
> .org/pal:/MM9.3.1/TH-1951-21742-22837-88?cc=1447693&wc=1220
> 5332 : downloaded 1 August 2012), for "Maine, Aroostook County
> Deed Books, 1865–1900," Southern Registry, vol. 51, image 101.

15. Point your Web browser to http://archive.quincylibrary.org/Default/
Skins/QPL/Client.asp?skin=QPL&AppName=2&AW=1343593579035,
click "Advanced Archive Search," search the *Quincy Daily Herald*
for "Edison," and write a double long-form reference-note citation
documenting the physical source and digital image that you see.

> "Boyhood of Edison: Something About the Youth of the Great
> Inventor," *Quincy Daily Herald*, Quincy, Ill., 24 August 1893,
> page 6, cols. 2–4; digital image, "Quincy Historic Newspaper
> Archive," *Quincy Public Library* (http://archive.quincylibrary
> .org/Default/Skins/QPL/Client.asp?skin=QPL&AppName=2&
> AW=1205417717890 : viewed 1 August 2012), advanced search for
> "Edison" in *The Quincy Daily Herald*.

Chapter 5 exercise answers

1. Using the Bible record citation in appendix B, note 2, and the image from that source . . . , answer the following analysis questions:

   a. Is the source an authored work, original record, or derivative record?

   This likely is a derivative record. The 1871–88 (and perhaps 1893) entries seem to have been written at one time, suggesting the page was copied from another record.

   b. Is the record's informant known? If so, who is it?

   Likely Ida, who owned the Bible and who would have been present at all the recorded events

   c. Is the information about Earl McLain's birth date primary information, secondary information, or indeterminable?

   Primary information, if Ida was the informant, which seems likely

   d. Suppose your research question is *When was Earl McLain born?* Does this source provide direct, indirect, or negative evidence? What answer does that evidence provide?

   Direct evidence—the information specifies that Earl was born on "Feb. 4th 1876."

   e. Suppose your research question is *When did Ida divorce Charles D. McLain?* Does this source provide direct, indirect, or negative evidence? What answer does that evidence provide?

   Indirect evidence. Earl's surname, his birth date, and Ida's second marriage date—without mentioning the divorce—provide the answer "The divorce occurred between 4 February 1876 and 29 March 1878."

    f. Why was this source created?

       It was created to record family members' births and marriages.

    g. Was there a time lapse between Earl's birth and this source's creation? Why do you think so?

       Yes, because Ida apparently wrote all the entries after 1888, perhaps after 1893.

    h. Was the record keeper careful?

       Probably

    i. Was the source open to challenge, verification, or correction?

       Probably not

    j. Was the source protected against bias, fraud, and tampering?

       Probably not

    k. Was the informant reliable as both observer and reporter, or did he or she show potential for bias or other factors affecting reliability?

       If Ida conceived Jesse before she divorced McLain, she could have falsified her second marriage date, Jesse's birth date, or both

    l. What do your answers tell you about this source's usefulness and credibility as a provider of genealogical evidence?

       It has hallmarks of reliability, but it shouldn't be completely trusted.

2. Use the form . . . to construct a table correlating evidence of names, ages, occupations, and birthplaces from the two census images. . . . Then comment on what the correlated evidence reveals about identities, relationships, and migration.

1850 CENSUS (MISSOURI)	1860 CENSUS (ILLINOIS)
Don Higele, born in Germany in 1811–12, *bricklayer*	*Antoine Higley, born in Hanover in 1809–10,* *Stone Mason*
Barb Higele, born in Germany in 1825–26	*Barbra Higley, born in Hanover in 1826–27*
Ad Higele, born in Germany in 1844–45	*Adolph Higley, born in Hanover in 1845–46*
Fritz Higele, born in Germany in 1845–46	*Fred[eric]k Higley, born in Hanover in 1846–47*
Joh[n?] Higele, born in Missouri, in 1847–48	
Marie Higele, born in Missouri in 1849–50	*Mary Higley, born in Illinois in 1849–50*
Corn Higele, born in Germany in 1826–27, bricklayer	
	Sopha Higley, born in Hanover in 1850–51
	Jacob Higley, born in Illinois in 1853–54
	Louisa Higley, born in Illinois in 1856–57

Commentary:

Although names, residences, and some details vary, the two censuses seem to identify one family. Don's name may have been recorded incorrectly in one of the censuses, or he may have changed his first name between 1850 and 1860. Specifics of his occupation vary but are compatible. He and his wife seem to have had two children (Adolph and Frederick) born in Hanover in the mid-1840s, two children born in Missouri in the late 1840s and perhaps 1850 (John and Mary), two children born in Illinois in the mid-1850s (Jacob and Louisa), and a daughter Sopha (Sophia?) likely born in Missouri or Illinois in 1850–51.

Don seems to have left Hanover with a wife and two sons between 1845 and 1849, when they were in Missouri. The family seems to have moved to Illinois between 1850 and 1854, perhaps between 1850 and 1851.

"Corn" (Cornelius?) may have been Don's brother—their ages are in range for brothers and they had the same occupation in 1850. "Corn" may have remained in Missouri, moved elsewhere, or died between 1850 and 1860. The apparent son John likely died between 1850 and 1860.

The 1850 census reports "Germany" as family members' birthplace, but it could mean anywhere in German-speaking Europe, since Germany did not exist as a unified country in 1850 or beforehand. Hanover might be correct or an error.

The two censuses seem consistent on the time of the move from Missouri to Illinois (Mary's 1850 enumeration in Missouri suggests her Illinois birthplace is unlikely. Sopha's birth between children born in America suggests her Hanover birthplace is unlikely). The censuses also are consistent on the three eldest children's birth years, suggesting the ages are correct. Mary's and Sopha's implausible birthplaces in 1860 and the seeming rounding of Antoine's age that year suggest the 1850 informant was more knowledgeable than the 1860 informant.

3. Following the model, use the article in appendix A to identify an example of each correlation format . . . showing points of agreement or disagreement and to comment on conclusions that each correlation supports or negates.

TYPE	LOCATION IN ARTICLE AND CONTENT	COMMENTS ON CONCLUSIONS
Narrative	The article's page 29, bottom of page; compares census and tax lists	Tax lists and censuses agree on Philip's approximate age.
Narrative	The article's pages 31–33 (Fairfax County tax lists, chain carrier, lessor, road orders, and Kentucky tax lists) show Philip lived in Fairfax County from at least 1786 through 1793–95, when he moved to Kentucky [*The article contains further examples of narrative correlations that would be correct answers.*]	All the correlated sources consistently support the conclusion that Philip lived in Fairfax County from before 1786 through 1793–95.
List	Bulleted list on pages 35–36. The first bullet compares Lewis's baptismal date with the court case, 1810 census, and tax records of Philip's age. The second bullet compares four sources concerning Lewis's death and heirs. [*The article contains further examples of list correlations that would be correct answers.*]	The correlated sources consistently support the conclusion that Philip and the Fairfax County Lewis Pritchett were not son and father
Timeline	The article's pages 36–37, the timeline concerning the senior Lewis Pritchett in three Virginia counties	The timeline is consistent for one adult male who could have been Philip Pritchett's father. It suggests he married twice (wives Mary and Jane). It also shows his move from Stafford County to Prince William County (in an area that later became Fauquier County) and his return a few years later to Stafford County
Table	The article's page 34, table 1, which compares land tax payments year by year for Lewis Pritchett and Lewis Pritchett "Junr."	The comparison shows that two Lewis Pritchett landowners lived in the county at the same time, and it matches the landholdings to each. Narrative text correlates the table with personal-property tax lists, showing the younger landowner lived elsewhere
Map	The article's page 32, figure 1, which compares five land records and an atlas	Establishes that Lewis Pritchett in Stafford County was more likely than Fairfax County's Lewis Pritchett to have participated in the Fauquier County lawsuit

4. Following the model, use the article in appendix B to identify an example of each correlation format discussed in this chapter showing points of agreement or disagreement and to comment on conclusions that each correlation supports or negates.

TYPE	LOCATION IN ARTICLE AND CONTENT	COMMENTS ON CONCLUSIONS
Narrative	The first paragraph under "Another Woman's Husband" on the article's pages 105–6 compares direct and negative evidence from the 1900 census with direct evidence from Charles and Ida's marriage record.	The discussion shows points of both agreement and disagreement between the two sources. Evidence elsewhere in the article shows the two sources pertain to the same man.
Narrative	The article's pages 107–8, under "A Man with Another Name," compare evidence from two Ancestry World Tree contributions with evidence from Ancestral File, five censuses, and Charles's marriage and death records.	The discussion shows points of both agreement and disagreement between the two sources. Evidence elsewhere in the article shows the two sources pertain to the same man.
List	The bulleted list on page 107 compares several sources providing evidence of Ida's husband and Emma's husband. [*The lists on pages 114–16 and 117 also correlate evidence from various sources and would be correct answers.*]	The correlation establishes that Ida's ex-husband subsequently married Emma.
Timeline	The timeline on the article's pages 109–10 and 112–14 correlates numerous sources concerning James McLain.	The correlation presents the details discussed on pages 114–17 supporting the conclusion that James's son was husband of both Emma and Ida.
Table	Table 1, page 105, correlates evidence from five censuses. [Table 3 *would be another correct answer.*]	The correlation reveals inconsistencies across censuses. It also shows parallels and inconsistencies between Ida's husband and Emma's husband.
Map	The map on page 103 shows six southwestern Michigan Counties with records of Ida's husband Charles D. McLain, Emma's husband Charles D. McLain, and James McLain and his relatives, including his son, David R. McLain.	The correlation shows that records of Ida's husband in Muskegon, Allegan, and Van Buren counties are near records of Emma's husband in Van Buren, Kent, and Newaygo counties. It also shows that both sets are records are near records of James McLain and his family in Ottawa, Kent, and Newaygo counties.

Chapter 6 exercise answers

1. What is the definition of conflicting evidence?

    Conflicting evidence items provide incompatible answers to the same question.

2. Why does genealogical proof require us to resolve conflicts with a conclusion?

    If we cannot resolve the conflict, we have no case for proof. A proved conclusion rests on all valid applicable evidence resulting from a thorough search, not part of it.

    [Chapter 6 exercise answers continue on next page.]

3. Following the model, place in the table below the elements of the following conflict-resolution discussions from the articles in appendixes A and B and circle the likely-correct answer that the conflict resolution supports:

a. The article in appendix B, paragraph at the top of its page 106 (2 conflicts)

b. The article in appendix A, the discussion under "Supporting Conclusion 4," on its pages 35–36

c. The article in appendix A, the discussion under "Supporting Conclusion 6," on its page 37

d. The article in appendix A, the discussion on page 37, the third bullet

e. The article in appendix B, the figure and discussion at the top of its page 112

f. The article in appendix B, its page 108, the point concerning Charles's mother's name; including the supporting timeline on the article's pages 109–14 and some of the bullet points on its pages 114–16

ONE SIDE OF CONFLICT	OPPOSING SIDE OF CONFLICT	KINDS OF EVIDENCE IN CONFLICT	WAY(S) CONFLICT IS RESOLVED
a1. Charles was born in January 1854 [for the resolution, see the article's page 119]	Charles was born in 1848–49	Direct versus direct	No corroboration for 1848–49; explanation
a2. Emma's husband was not previously married	Emma married Ida's ex-husband	Direct versus indirect	No corroboration; quality of evidence; explanation
b. Philip's father was Lewis Pritchett of Fairfax County	Philip's father was not Lewis Pritchett of Fairfax County	Indirect versus direct and negative	No corroboration; documented explanation of who Lewis's children were
c. Lewis of Fairfax County represented Philip in his 1783 lawsuit	Lewis of Stafford County represented Philip in the lawsuit	Indirect versus Indirect	Explanation of proximity and custom
d. Phebe was enumerated with *David* "McLane"	Phebe was enumerated with *Daniel* "McLane"	Indirect versus direct	Explanation of handwriting and copying; no corroboration for *Daniel*
e. Charles's mother was Mary Mapes	Charles's mother was Phebe Wright	Direct versus indirect	Lack of corroboration for *Mary*, explanation; indirect evidence supporting *Phebe*

4. Propose and explain a resolution to the following conflicting evidence of Charles Jones's birth date. Mention in your explanation the kind(s) of evidence in conflict and the kind(s) of resolutions you used:

BIRTH-DATE EVIDENCE	SOURCES
1839–40	Federal censuses of 1900, 1910, and 1920
22 September 1841	Charles's wife's family Bible and his pension application, death certificate, and two gravestones
1841–42	Federal census of 1880
After March 1842	March 1856 court case in which Charles was disqualified from testifying because he was under age fourteen; his older sister and two uncles gave evidence in the case
1843–44	Federal censuses of 1850, 1860, and 1870
1843–47	Charles's mother's 1853 letter saying he had started school and could "read and writt [sic] very well"
1844–45	1861 enlistment date and family lore that he enlisted at age sixteen

Resolution and explanation:

Charles was born in 1843–44. The court case, an original record with primary information created in an open court with an impartial judge and the presence of three people likely knowledgeable of Charles's birth or age, is difficult to dispute. It therefore rules out the 1839–41 birth dates, which come from secondary information or unknown informants. The court case and mother's letter—another eyewitness account in an original record—agree on a date within 1843–47. The 1850, 1860, and 1870 federal censuses, the earliest in Charles's life when his age would be less vulnerable to error, agree with each other that he was born in 1843–44, a range compatible with both the court information and the mother's letter.

This is a conflict between direct evidence and indirect evidence. (Information in all but three sources provide direct evidence. The mother's letter and the sources for "1844–45" provide indirect evidence.) The resolution is based on the qualities of the evidence.

[Chapter 6 exercise answers continue on next page.]

5. Which of the five methods of assembling evidence listed on this book's pages 77–78 was used to support the conclusion *the widow of Lewis "Pritchart" was Frances*? See the article in appendix A, its page 35, bullet 2, and footnotes 27–29. Explain your answer.

> *Number 1: Direct evidence and no conflict.*
>
> *The order to sell slaves provides direct evidence of Lewis's widow's name. Lewis's absence from the 1802 tax list (negative evidence) coinciding with Frances's appearance in that list (indirect evidence) agrees with the direct evidence. No known evidence conflicts with this conclusion.*

6. Which of the five methods of assembling evidence was used to support the conclusion *the parents of Philip Pritchett who died in Kentucky in 1811–12 were Lewis and Mary (Lattimore) Pritchett of Stafford and Fauquier counties, Virginia.* See appendix A, the entire article. Explain your answer.

> *Number 5: Resolved conflicting indirect evidence and an absence of direct evidence.*
>
> *No source concerning Philip identifies his parents directly, and no source concerning Lewis and Mary specifies directly that they had a son Philip. The case is made primarily from indirect evidence from land and tax records. Conflicts arise from indirect evidence as well: his association with Lewis Pritchett in Fairfax County suggests that Lewis was his father; Philip's signing a petition in 1781 suggests he was too old to be a minor in the 1783 court case. Evidence showing the Fairfax County Lewis had no son Philip and explanation resolve the first conflict. Explanation resolves the second conflict.*

7. Which of the five methods of assembling evidence was used to support the conclusion *the parents of Ida Tucker's first husband, Charles D. McLain, were James and Phebe McLain.* See appendix B, the entire article. Explain your answer.

> *Number 5: Resolved conflicting indirect evidence and an absence of direct evidence.*
>
> *No source naming Ida and her first husband, Charles D., also names his parents. No source naming James and Phebe says they had a son Charles. The case is made from indirect evidence from censuses, pension application files, and other sources. Conflicts arise in the name of James and Phebe's son, David R., and discrepancies in his and Ida's husband's ages. Those conflicts are resolved with explanation and many indirect evidence items showing that Charles D. and David R. McLain were the same person.*

Chapter 7 exercise answers

1. Locate three proof statements in the article in appendix A. State the conclusion that each statement proves.

   "Philip 'Pritchartt' died in Montgomery County, Kentucky, between 10 November 1811 and 10 March 1812" (the article's page 29, under "A Virginian in Kentucky")

   Philip was born "between September 1762 and 6 August 1765" (the article's page 30, bullet 3).

   "In 1782 and 1783 two Lewis Pritchetts owned land in Stafford County" (the article's page 33, under "Supporting Conclusion 2").

   [Many other examples in this article also would be correct choices.]

2. Locate two proof summaries in the article in appendix A. State the conclusion that each summary proves.

   Philip lived in Fairfax County (the article's pages 31–33, under "Supporting Conclusion 1").

   Philip was not the son of Lewis Pritchett of Fairfax County ("Young Lewis") (pages 35–36, under "Supporting Conclusion 4).

   [Conclusions under each of the article's five other "Supporting Conclusion" subheads also would be correct choices.]

3. Describe the "beginning" of the proof-argument article in appendix A.

   The article's "beginning" covers its pages 29–30 and the first paragraph on its page 31. This section identifies the primary research subject, puts him in geographic and chronological contexts, describes the research problem and context, and answers the research question.

4. Describe the "end" of the proof-argument article in appendix A.

> *The article's "end" is the bottom half of its page 38 under "Conclusion."*
> *It summarizes the case's conclusion and the process of its determination.*

5. List two approaches the author of the proof argument/article in appendix B uses to develop the argument's "middle." Explain or give an example of each.

> *Building blocks. The identification of Ida's husband lays the foundation.*
> *This transitions to the identification of Emma's husband and then James*
> *and Phebe's son. These building blocks lead to the conclusion that the son*
> *and both husbands were one person.*
>
> *Single hypothesis. The entire article addresses the hypothesis that Ida's*
> *husband, Emma's husband, and James and Phebe's son were the same*
> *person. This hypothesis is suggested at the bottom of the article's page 108*
> *and made explicit from its page 114 through the end of the article.*

6. Select a genealogical article of interest to you that you believe is a proof argument. [Via the NGS website's members-only area, NGS members may download *NGS Quarterly* articles back through 1979; everyone will find a short selection of genealogical articles and proof arguments online at "Sample Work Products," *Board for Certification of Genealogists* (http://www.bcgcertification.org/skillbuilders/worksamples.html). You also may select articles from elsewhere.] Use your selected article to respond to the following [parts a–g]:

> *Answers to question 6, parts a–g, will vary with the article or proof*
> *argument you select.*

Chapter 8 exercise answers

> *Answers to chapter 8 exercises will vary with the material you select.*